D1742474

REVELATIONS FROM MY BEDSIDE

A Collection of Inspirational Narratives

JULLET SIMPSON

authorHOUSE®

AuthorHouse™ UK
1663 Liberty Drive
Bloomington, IN 47403 USA
www.authorhouse.co.uk
Phone: UK TFN: 0800 0148641 (Toll Free inside the UK)
*   UK Local: (02) 0369 56322 (+44 20 3695 6322 from outside the UK)*

© 2021 Jullet Simpson. All rights reserved.

No part of this book may be reproduced, stored in a retrieval system, or transmitted by any means without the written permission of the author.

Published by AuthorHouse   11/29/2021

ISBN: 978-1-6655-9460-8 (sc)
ISBN: 978-1-6655-9459-2 (e)

Library of Congress Control Number: 2021922839

Print information available on the last page.

Any people depicted in stock imagery provided by Getty Images are models, and such images are being used for illustrative purposes only. Certain stock imagery © Getty Images.

This book is printed on acid-free paper.

Because of the dynamic nature of the Internet, any web addresses or links contained in this book may have changed since publication and may no longer be valid. The views expressed in this work are solely those of the author and do not necessarily reflect the views of the publisher, and the publisher hereby disclaims any responsibility for them.

Scriptures marked KJV are taken from the KING JAMES VERSION (KJV): KING JAMES VERSION, public domain.

To my parents, Pastor Richard and Myrtle Simpson, who are awaiting the first resurrection of Jesus Christ.

My mum always used to say that I was 'an explorer'.

CONTENTS

ACKNOWLEDGEMENTS

FIRSTLY, I WOULD LIKE to give my heavenly Father special thanks for the opportunity to pen these writings that he inspired me to collate and write over the years. He spoke to my heart about them and he deserves all the praise and glory for the outcome.

Thank you, Bev Roberts-Bailey, for your advice of 'write, sit down and relax with a drink', when checking the document. It worked for me.

Thank you, Father for my Christian parents, who both raised me up in the fear of the Lord, and for their godly example of living a holy life. They are no longer here, but their legacy lives on.

Ruth Addo, for your initial pair of eyes on the first story. Your time, and advice was very much appreciated.

And finally, I would like to thank and acknowledge the editorial team of Authorhouse UK; especially all those involved in the whole production of making this book possible. Thank you for believing in me, and giving me the opportunity to be a part of your publishing world family. For your kind support along the way I thank you Jennifer Dominise, May Arado, and Philip Clarkson.

PREFACE

B EING THE DAUGHTER OF a well-known pastor seemed to mean that I automatically showed some promise as a speaker. Sometimes, I would be called upon to share a message, or give a sermon. Having listened to so many sermons in my life, I wanted to explore different themes and concepts that I had not heard before. I took it upon myself to search the scriptures to learn more, because I was spiritually hungry and curious. As an avid reader, I read through the Bible, and browsed through biblical concordances and commentaries to see what I would discover.

It was at my bedside as I kneeled, meditating upon the scriptures, that the Lord poured out these different thoughts and ideas about the characters mentioned in this book. I wanted to get into their heads to fully appreciate and understand their experiences and how it shaped their own lives. I was particularly intrigued by the lives of Leah and Michal; two individuals whose lives were over-shadowed by their more popular husbands Jacob and David, respectively.

Over the years, I have had the chance to share a few of my messages. Many of them lay untouched until fairly recently in 2018. The Lord also revealed to me that I would one day write a book and I believe that time has come.

I wrote this book in order to showcase some of the characters in the Bible that I found of great interest, and to give them centre stage. And, of course, I want to share some of my writings with you. May the Holy Spirit illumine your heart as you read this collection of narratives. Let the words find meaning and healing to your soul. Finally, I pray that they will bless, uplift and inspire you. In Jesus's name.

CONFRONTING YOUR GARRISONS

WHAT IS A GARRISON? A garrison is a fortified military base or headquarters that is protected and staffed by troops or soldiers at a location such as a town, city, fort, ship, or castle. It is kept under high security and constantly maintained. It may be positioned in a neighbouring nation or country that may be a friend or, more likely, a foe.

From a spiritual perspective, a garrison may be regarded as a form of fear or a problem that causes other strongholds to be fortified within the mind. The emotions of doubt, stress, and anxiety may also develop, causing an individual to lose self-control, creating emotional instability and ultimately damaging one's overall health and well-being. The garrison is thus maintained and fed by negative ideas and external influences.

Circumstances may contribute to making a garrison present within an individual's life. Situations such as ill health, depression, lifestyle choices, toxic or dysfunctional relationships, and poor self-esteem may trigger low confidence. These situations may also cause a person to lash out and make costly mistakes as a result of irrational thinking.

This lesson will look at how to identify and deal with garrisons or strongholds by examining five mistakes that King Saul made when dealing with situations mentioned in 1 Samuel 13.

1. The Garrison of Premature Celebrations

Do not boast or advertise your victories prematurely until your garrisons or strongholds have been completely dealt with.

In 1 Samuel 13:3, Saul's eldest son, Jonathan, singlehandedly attacked the garrison of the Philistines, stationed in Geba in the geographical area near Gibeah, and killed many men. Jonathan routed ten thousand and put them to flight. The Philistines had knowledge of this and did not immediately retaliate.

But Saul, wanting to add insult to injury, blew a trumpet and advertised the news of his son's triumph throughout the entire Israelite camp. The information of the trumpet reached the ears of their enemies. The Israelite camp became offensive to the Philistines, who immediately rounded up a force comprising thirty thousand chariots, six thousand horsemen, and countless other fighters against Saul's pathetic army of just three thousand men.

Those sorts of victories are worth bragging about. But it was not the right thing to do on this occasion, when in their immediate camp they had only three thousand men, compared to an enemy who are described as 'people like the sand of the sea'. Their bragging certainly would have annoyed the enemy.

Sometimes you just have be silent and find some other occasion to celebrate—preferably in the peace of your hometown, away from the enemy's camp. Jonathan was smart enough to keep his mouth shut. But Jonathan's father not only blurted out the victory but also took the credit for it! As king, blowing the trumpet (or his voice) prematurely throughout the land led to his own embarrassment and demise.

2. The Garrison of Cowardice

Face your fears and do not run away.

According to 1 Samuel 13:6, when the men of Israel saw they

were in difficulty, the people were distressed and hid themselves in caves and thickets, amongst the rocks, in high places, and in pits.

Imagine, your enemies have camped in your territory and are forcing you out by their sheer presence! It doesn't help if you're already afraid. So naturally, on that kind of low energy your body's primary response is to physically withdraw to get away from it all and find refuge outside. Anywhere away from your enemies.

As humans, we are prone to failure and anxiety. In any situation where we are outnumbered, we must muster courage and wait upon the Lord, and allow him to fight our battles: 'Wait on the Lord, be of good courage and he shall strengthen thine heart' (Psalm 27:14).

In 1 Samuel 13:7, some of the Hebrews go over Jordan to Gad and Gilead. As for Saul, he was still in Gilgal, and all the people followed behind him, trembling. The people felt very vulnerable, defenceless, helpless, and defeated, as they had no weapons to fight back with.

What is interesting but sad here is Saul's inability as a leader to make any real attempt to motivate or uplift the people. He didn't encourage the people to put their trust in God. As king, he failed to inspire hope or confidence within his men. They continued to follow him in fear and trepidation.

The scriptures do not suggest that he went off to pray and seek God's face for direction, nor that he asked a priest for the ephod, or the Urim and Thummim. As a result, some of the people made up their own minds in favour of self-preservation and just left him.

When faced with the prospect of problems too large to solve, some people will disappear from your life. Some people hang around only until bad circumstances surface.

3. The Garrison of Disobedience

Follow and obey the instructions of the Lord.

Under the strict instructions of the prophet Samuel, Saul was commanded to remain in Gilgal until Samuel returned to offer sacrifices for his inauguration as king. Whilst he was waiting, even more people started to leave him.

Saul's impatience caused his disobedience. He panicked because the people were falling away. So he presumptuously assumed the priestly role and offered up the burnt offering in a ritual meant only for Samuel, as priest, to perform.

Desperate people do desperate things. But it was an unwise move, especially at the risk of displeasing God. This action forfeited Saul's right as king: 'And Samuel said to Saul, You have done foolishly: you should have kept the commandment of the Lord your God which he commanded you: for now the Lord would have established your kingdom upon Israel forever. But now your kingdom shall not continue' (1 Samuel 13:13).

Disobedience to God is equated to witchcraft.

4.   The Garrison of Blame

Take responsibility for your actions.

When asked why he offered up the sacrifice instead of waiting for Samuel, Saul had a million and one excuses. Some of these are as follows:

- 'I saw. I panicked. The people scarpered.'
- 'You didn't turn up at the time appointed.'
- 'The Philistines are at Michmash.'
- 'I haven't made supplication, or entreated the face of God.'
- 'I forced myself to make an offering to God.'

Unfortunately, Saul forgot that the same God who had made him king was able to deliver whenever possible. Saul had a 'people' mentality that pointed the finger away from his own crimes and towards others. The situation was for him as a king to manage. The resources were there, and God was just a prayer away.

Saul's original army of three thousand men was now reduced to a paltry six hundred war-weary warriors. When we do the maths, that amounts to two thousand four hundred men who walked away from Saul within a short time.

If a situation arises where enemies overwhelm your circumstances, remember your past victories that Jesus has given and the stories of deliverance in the Word, such as Elisha and his servant with the armies of the Lord (2 Kings 6:13–17).

5. The Garrison of Exposed Weaknesses

Defend and protect your territory or boundaries.

In 1 Samuel 13:17–18, three groups of spoilers emerge from the camp of the Philistines, one heading to Orphah in Shual in the northern area, a second to Beth-Horon in the central area, and the third to the Zeboim valley, a wilderness to the south of the region. This passage reveals the strategy of Israel's enemy. As the land of Israel was deserted by its people in fear and discouragement, the Philistines were able to easily gain access to Israel's crops, belongings, and possessions.

The enemies struck at the headquarters in Orphah, situated north of Benjamin. Another group targeted Beth-Horon, west of Benjamin; and the third group raided Zeboim, south of Benjamin. Top, middle, and bottom—this would mean utter desolation and destruction. 'The thief comes not just to steal but also to kill and destroy' (John 10:10).

As with facing literal enemies, those who leave their discernment behind them or allow their personal vulnerabilities to be exposed attract enemies who will exploit the situation without their knowledge. This opens these people to manipulative control, intimidation, criticism, and being taken advantage of. When a person is too busy running away to hide and to emotionally protect himself from being hurt, the inability to deal with the problem can become quite stressful and too much to cope with.

Do not leave your emotional borders—such as your weaknesses, vulnerabilities, and trusting nature—open to your enemies. Keep your inner life closed from those whose only aim is to mess with your mind psychologically or emotionally by draining you, stressing you, and causing you to fret. Spiritually, this harassment can even make you doubt God, thus reducing your ability to fight your own battles.

Satan uses all manner of proven techniques to wear down even a seasoned Christian. One of these techniques is depression. He will attack the mind, bombarding it with negative thoughts, or even use fellow Christians to taunt you, causing emotional upheaval or physical and spiritual depression. It's important that you have a battle plan from God, as the devil has a take-no-prisoners policy!

If your mind is empty, the devil will fill it up with all kinds of ungodly rubbish—things that do not edify the soul—when you have nothing to combat or counteract it. Be reminded to 'Let the word of God dwell in you richly in all wisdom; teaching and admonishing one another in psalms and hymns and spiritual songs, singing with grace in your hearts to the Lord' (Colossians 3:16).

Do not allow yourself to be manipulated or controlled by the enemy. Do not allow yourself to be wholly dependent on friends or people, because they will eventually fall short or let you down. Put your trust in the Lord.

In verses 19–23, the Philistines make the Hebrews dependent upon them. This was a cruel and embarrassing dilemma. They had no craftsmen or smiths available amongst them, thus placing them in a very awkward situation. They were forced to approach their enemies' territory to sharpen their agricultural tools, which were fit only for their fields.

The Philistines knew that the Israelites were at a loss and used that to their advantage. The agricultural tools were of no use for war, but just for ploughing the earth. How ridiculous! By being disempowered, the Israelites were enslaved to baser equipment.

Spiritual insight: Never allow yourself to be dependent upon another individual's skill or gift. Don't bow to someone else's level.

One tool that was available to the Israelites was a mattock, which is a type of large pick that has a blade at one end shaped like an adze, attached at right angles, used for dressing timber, loosening soil, and cutting roots.

Another type of farming tool was a coulter, which has a blade or sharp-edged disc attached to a plough so that it cuts through soil vertically in front of the ploughshare.

Axes, mattocks, forks, and coulters will not help you win physical battles. Carnal weapons cannot be employed when engaging in spiritual combat. The only persons with spears and swords were Saul and his son. It was a pitiful and embarrassing situation to be in.

The Israelites were operating from a position of powerlessness and were dependent upon their enemy's smiths to whet their agricultural tools. The Philistines gladly obliged in whetting the tools of the Israelites, because they knew that these tools were not only worthless but also useless for combat in the battle.

'The weapons of our warfare are mighty through God to pulling down of strongholds' (1 Corinthians 4:3–4). When fighting our battles, we must be equipped with the correct tools to make an impact.

Spiritual battles must be fought with the spiritual weapons, as listed in Ephesian 6:10–16, to defeat our enemies. What is the use of wearing armour without the appropriate weapon with which to engage in combat!

shield—faith,	belt—truth	sword—Word of God/Spirit
shoe—peace	helmet—salvation	cloak—zeal and prayer

Each piece is integral to the others. Be harnessed and armoured in the righteousness of God.

It is time for us to recognize who our enemies are and not conform to their way of living. Be prepared to confront sin. We may have internal 'philistines', which are constant irritants to the inner man. These philistines are the works of the flesh that wage against our members, as children of God. We cannot allow them to gain permanent prominence in our lives. We need to remain in constant in seeking, reading, and godly living to reduce the pride, anger, and hypocrisy from our lives and win the battle of the mind.

Identifying our garrisons, or strongholds, needs to be done with the aid of the Holy Spirit, with brutal honesty and scrutiny of the self. The mirror of God's Word will reveal where we go wrong, along with the corrective measures needed to ensure both discipline and sanctification.

Some of the types of garrisons (or strongholds), include the following:

fear	jealousy	clinginess/ neediness	control
anxiety	hatred	critical spirit	resentment
depression	malice	pride	guilt
anger	insecurity	slander	hopelessness
bitterness	resentfulness	gossip	helplessness

Let's take a look at the trait of jealousy. It is an emotion which has many attachments. It has a proven formula:

What it is: A poisonous, toxic personality trait	Jealousy= Lousy zeal Jealousy consumes and destroys lives and relationships.	Traits associated with it: Insincerity Maliciousness Insecurity Possessiveness Fear Bitterness Control (or loss of control) Pride Hatred Envy Covetousness Anger Strife Murder	'It is as cruel a the grave; the coals thereof are coals of fire, which are a most vehement flame.' (Song of Solomon 8:6)

8

When jealousy becomes a stronghold in your life, it not only affect you, but also adversely affects others around you. We can harbour a tendency to be jealous in relationships, but it rarely has a good ending. Jealousy is a sign of immaturity, which strangles growth and healthy communication, and causes issues regarding intimacy and trust. This particular garrison leaves devastation and destruction in its path for any individual involved. If not properly dealt with, it causes relationships to smoulder to ashes.

Using the above formula to deal with jealousy as a garrison, we must confront it, recognize the issue for what it is, and confess that it is a problem that needs to be eliminated from your life. Don't brag about it. It's not an attractive quality and doesn't produce lasting relationships. Obey the Word of God, which encourages us to love and not hate. Don't blame other people; be responsible for your own actions. Do all you can to protect good living with the tools God has equipped you with.

In our spiritual toolbox, we must incorporate mature agape love, sensitivity, active listening skills, discretion, and discernment in understanding how to deal with this ugly trait. When all else fails, you must know when to walk away and terminate the relationship. It is most important to walk away when the two parties are not working off the same page.

Saul's 'flaw' crops up again in chapter 15 in verses 9, 15, and 20. Do not use people as an excuse for your own blunders. God holds us all accountable when he asks for our obedience and adherence to his commands.

People may be manipulative, opinionated, critical, and decisive on your behalf. But remember: we must fully trust the Lord. 'Lean not on your own understanding. In all your ways acknowledge him and he'll direct your paths' (Proverbs 3:5).

Let us remember to deal with our spiritual garrisons so we can ride out every circumstance that life may present to us. Confronting such circumstances is much better than passive defeat.

DANIEL'S DEN OF LIONS

DANIEL WAS BORN OF noble Jewish descent from the royal tribe of Judah. During the early reign of king Jehoiakim, he was taken captive to Babylon by Nebuchadnezzar, king of Babylon, aged approximately seventeen years old, where he was trained for service.

In the book of Daniel, chapter 1, verses 3-4, we are told that

Ashpenaz should bring certain of the children of Israel, and of the king's seed, and of the princes; Children in whom there is no blemish, but well-favoured, and skilful in all wisdom, and cunning in knowledge, and understanding science, and such as had ability in them to stand in the king's palace, and whom they might teach the learning and the tongue of the Chaldeans.

Daniel fulfilled the criteria of overall excellence. He was given a new name, Belteshazzar, and a new identity, with an opportunity to serve a foreign king - who served foreign idols - and to learn the language and culture of his new home.

Alongside him were three other youths, named Hananiah, Mishael, and Azariah, who were also taken into captivity to serve the king. Their names were changed to Shadrach, Meshach, and Abednego, respectively. These young men were also made eunuchs, which although the bible does not suggest that they were castrated, married or had any children, they lived a eunuch-like lifestyle. They were to stand before the king as his advisors and counsellors. This would be equivalent to the Prime Minister having a dedicated team of civil servants, and ministers with various skill sets at hand when required.

One of the first obstacles they were confronted with was in the matter regarding food and drinks. The king requested that all his new subjects share the same royal diet that he was accustomed to and enjoyed. Daniel stood up for his principles and negotiated with their attendant, Melzar, who agreed to a stipulated ten-day diet of just fruits and vegetables. If they looked healthy after that time, then those meals would continue. This agreement would prevent them from having to eat from off the king's personal menu, which was probably blessed by their nation's gods.

Verses 17-20 states,

As for these four children, God gave them knowledge and skill in all learning and wisdom: and Daniel had understanding in all visions and dreams. At the end of the days that the king had said he should bring them in, then the prince of the eunuchs brought them in before Nebuchadnezzar. And the king communed with them; and among them all was none like them. And in all matters of wisdom and understanding, the king inquired of them, he found them ten times better than all the magicians and astrologers that were in all his realm.

The outcome was astounding. The faces of the youths were by far better and fairer in complexion, and to top things off, they were ten times more intelligent than the other magicians and astrologers who were officiating in Nebuchadnezzar's kingdom.

Daniel continued in his role as advisor even unto the first year of King Cyrus (around 605 BC.)

By chapter 5, Daniel was already established as a prophet who heard from God and a subject who was faithful and loyal to the kings he served. He revealed the dream about the metal man image, which none of the other court magicians and astrologers were able to do. He also revealed the meaning of the dream, which foretold that Nebuchadnezzar would be driven into the field to eat grass like oxen, wet with the dew of heaven, seven times until he recognized that the Most High rules in the kingdom of men and 'giveth it to whomsoever he will' (Daniel 4:25).

He briefly served under Belshazzar, another king of Babylon.

This notoriously evil ruler also had a visitation from God, when he presumptuously took the dedicated vessels out of the temple of the house of God and drank wine out of them, celebrating the gods of gold, silver, brass, iron, wood, and stone. A hand appeared upon the wall and wrote a strange message in a language that no one could interpret. Daniel was recommended by the queen, who says in chapter 5, verse 10,

'Oh king, live for ever: let not your thoughts trouble you, nor let your countenance be changed: There is a man in your kingdom, in whom is the spirit of the holy gods; and in the days of your father light and understanding and wisdom, like the wisdom of the gods, was found in him; … your father made master of the magicians, astrologers, Chaldeans, and soothsayers; Forasmuch as an excellent spirit, and knowledge, and understanding interpreting of dreams, and showing of hard sentences, and dissolving of doubts, were found in the same Daniel …'

Armed with the revelation of God, Daniel revealed the difficult text 'Mene, Mene, Tekel, Uphasin', which had been written by God's hand mysteriously on the wall. Belshazzar's kingdom was finished, he was weighed in the balances and found lacking, and his kingdom was now being divided up between the Medes and Persians.

The Babylonian head of gold depicted in Nebuchadnezzar's dream was broken, and Daniel entered the next kingdom phase of silver, represented by the breasts and arms of the metal man, as found in Daniel chapter 2.

King Darius I was an acclaimed Median king who ascended to the throne at the age of sixty-two, in 522 BC. Based on an extract from Wikipedia,

He organized the empire by dividing it up into provinces and placed satraps to govern it. He organized Achaemenid coinage as a new uniform monetary system, along with making Aramaic the official language of the empire. He also put the empire in better standing by building roads and introducing standard weights and measures. Through these changes, the empire was centralized and unified. Darius also worked on construction projects throughout the empire focusing on Susa, Pasargadae, Babylon and Egypt.

It was in the face of this information that Daniel entered, and he was quite advanced in age but was still a seasoned, mature man of God who stood firm in his faith. He was about to be tested because the king wanted to promote him above the whole kingdom. It would look something like this:

King Darius 》	120 Satraps 》	First President—Daniel	Daniel to rule over the realm!
		Second President	
		Third President	

Although these men were already established in very powerful positions, they were still envious of Daniel and his close relationship with the king. They would have been well aware that he was a captive slave and a foreigner from the Jewish nation. Added to that knowledge, they had been acquainted with his successes in interpreting difficult dreams and visions, as well as his impressive work ethic. This man caught the king's eye because a spirit of excellence was found in him. He was faithful, loyal, and diligent in his administration and business. He daily balanced it by keeping his relationship with God fresh. We must remember that if he was to be married, that reality was removed the day he was made a eunuch.

The Position of the Satrap

The occupation of satrap was given to only the most elite of society. Daniel came from a noble bloodline, and the pagan kings were keen to invest in the best brains in their kingdoms. Satraps (also known as princes) were appointed by kings and were made heads of administration. They collected taxes, were given judicial authority, were responsible for internal security, and maintained armies.

The one hundred and twenty satraps employed under Darius were also in top prestigious positions of power which commanded honour and respect. The king was so impressed with Daniel's deportment that he wanted to promote him as head over the entire realm—over all the satraps and over the other presidents, of which he was one. If this was up for discussion amongst them, then they would have most likely secretly fumed at the proposal.

With this in mind, they began to plot Daniel's downfall. These intelligent men were so threatened by this outsider, who had served with true integrity towards God and king, that they now needed to examine the evidence. They somehow needed to find some fault or flaw in this individual to deem him unworthy for this new honorary position.

Enter the Lions

Metaphorically speaking, all the men at the top level of the governmental structure functioned as 'lions', meaning that they were leaders in positions of power, authority, and status. This included the king, from a monarchical point of view, plus the three presidents and the one hundred and twenty satraps just below him. They wielded enormous control and influence, so it was hard to see why they would become so envious or insecure of somebody else, given the choice positions they held.

Nonetheless, their envy spilled out into cruel hatred, and they needed to find a plausible reason to get rid of Daniel. They began to scrutinize his movements, padding around, checking out his work ethic, and speaking to other members to find out if there were any discrepancies regarding him. Daniel, as a managerial 'lion', was now the target to be eliminated. He was their prey. He was the hunted one.

Daniel was a good lion (leader), whilst the other men were evil lions. They were territorial and spent a lot of time together hatching plans on how to pull this righteous man down. You see, whilst he was on their level, they didn't care so much. But the very thought of being made accountable to him didn't sit well with them. Although we are not told what period of time they spent scrutinizing him, we are told that they could not find any fault or error in his job or in him as an individual. Every report came back as 'Excellent', 'Very good', 'Impressive', 'Exceptional', and 'Can't fault him'.

This really isn't new at all. These sorts of behaviour typically happen in the workplace environment, the church, or other social settings. In such scenarios, someone's jealousy causes him or her to create havoc or mischief in order to expose another and put him or her in a bad light. If there is a promotion available at work, there are people who will try to outshine you in their performance so they can sabotage your chances and thus achieve their ambition, especially if it looks as though you might win out. They will watch to see whether you make any mistakes so that they can report to management whilst watching their own backs and covering their tracks, just in case they get caught out.

Darius's Law

The plotters had to come up with a better plan. One day, during one of their discussions on how to 'eliminate' Daniel, they came up with a suggestion regarding his religion and personal relationship with God. They also looked at his relationship with the king and decided to make a decree that they hoped would drive a wedge in Daniel's life regarding the matter. These 'lions' began to scheme, and their spoken words soon became words on an important scroll. In their excitement, they had found the solution.

The presidents and the princes rushed in to have an audience with King Darius, and they told him that all the presidents of the kingdom, the governors, the princes, the counsellors, and the captains had consulted to establish a royal decree and were in full agreement on it. (Even today, a bill has to have the backing of many other supporters in order to substantiate it and make it lawful.) The decree stated, 'Whosoever shall ask a petition of any God or man for thirty days, except from the king, he [will] be cast into the lions' den.' The edict was simple, but the punishment was so severe. Surely, the king should have sensed that something was amiss.

Notice how all the presidents and satraps knew about the decree but deliberately excluded Daniel because it was only in regard to him. This was not about other people.

The decree would last for just one month, thus giving Daniel an opportunity to choose whom he would serve and obey—whether God or king. It was such a preposterous proposal to have people continually ask requests only from the king. But behind it lay devious motives. It would also give his conspirators the chance to finally flush this guy out of the kingdom once and for all. By appealing to the king's ego, the decree would essentially ruin Darius's relationship with his favourite right-hand man. Why? Because they knew that Daniel was a man of prayer.

With regard to the Medes and Persian laws, there was a rule specifying that laws could not be reversed once they were implemented, whether orally or written. There was no backtracking or changing of the laws which the king agreed to. Without hesitancy, and with little persuasion, Darius signed the papers, not fully realizing what he had actually done.

The First Lions' Den

Daniel was in his 'lions' den, which, in this case, was his immediate workplace surroundings. The 'lions' in this story are his work colleagues: the two other presidents and the one hundred and twenty satraps who were also involved in manufacturing his downfall. These 'lions' were two-footed, and their tactics were ferocious and deadly in nature.

Daniel's heroic character and faith were on trial, and he was not intimidated one little bit. As soon as he heard about the decree, he went up to his room as always with his windows opened towards Jerusalem and prayed on his knees, giving thanks to God.

What We Can Learn about Lions

Through an extract from the book *Lion Taming*, by Stephen L. Katz, we can determine the following: 'To lions, you are either prey, the enemy or ignored. They eat the prey, kill the enemy and disregard anyone of no value.' Some lions like to work alone, whilst others team up to kill. They can be ruthless, competitive, cunning, and cooperative. In order to survive, they need to plot strategically in order to catch their prey. Often, they will lurk in tall grass, padding slowly, carefully, and with precision to watch their intended meal. They will target their prey based on whether it is alone, weak, afraid, exposed, wounded, off-guard, unprotected, young, or vulnerable. Sometimes the prey is actually bigger than the lions, but with a little help from the pride, they are able to capture it and bring it down to the ground.

Lionesses are known to best work together as a team and share their spoils with the rest of the pride. They take no prisoners. They attack until the prey resists or die. They even mark their territory with urine to informing others that it is their domain. They use methods of confusion to make their prey think that they are not interested in attacking, but it's just a clever ploy. They will also engage others within the group to assist with the attack.

The impact lions have is centred on four important pillars:

> **Dominance**: Lions dominate through their sphere of authority, influence, and advantage. (The presidents wanted total control, with Daniel out of the picture.)
> **Social Standing**: This refers to the lion's status, ego, and self-image amongst others, and how the lion is regarded and treated. (They didn't like Daniel. He didn't fit in with them, and they didn't like the idea of him being over them.)
> **Territory**: Lions, like kings, protect, maintain, and retain the place from which they rule. (Daniel was a captive from Judah. Babylon was their territory, not his.)

> ➤ **Survival**: To lions, survival is the true mark of success. (If they worked together as one, then they could break the king's relationship with Daniel.)

In this story we can see some incredible similarities between the presidents' behaviour, and the traits of lions. Noticeably, these powerful 'lions' were jealous of Daniel because of their own insecurities. This, in turn, birthed seeds of bitterness within them, which grew and formed other offshoots of pride, resentment, hatred, wrath, malice, pretence, gossip, slander, insincerity, strife, scorn, deception, hypocrisy, and an inclination to murder.

There is strength in numbers, and unfortunately, these one hundred and twenty-two men teamed up with an ambition to destroy just one man, whose life shone brighter than theirs. What started as a vendetta for pride ended up with a lot of people calling for Daniel's blood.

Surprisingly, in the story, we don't get a glimpse of any conversations passing between Daniel and the other satraps, we get only their interactions between the king. A lot of the presidents' time was spent trying to destroy the reputation of this honourable man of God who served the king and the people.

The scriptures are abundant with verses that expose vicious enemies whose behaviour is likened to the animal characteristics of bulls, dogs, unicorns and lions. Comparing the attitudes of Daniel's work colleagues against the lions, Paul, in the book of Acts, mentions that 'God had stopped the lions' mouth'(11:33). King David, in one of his psalms, requested that God save him from the mouth of a lion. In both cases, these are references to people, not four-footed beasts.

The righteous are bold as a lion (Proverbs 28:1b)

(The above verse describes people being as brave as lions.)

Israel is a scattered sheep; the lions have driven him away: first the king of Assyria has devoured him; and last this Nebuchadrezzar king of Babylon has broken his bones. (Jeremiah 50:17)

(Prophetically speaking, the 'lions' in the above verse refer to the king of Assyria and King Nebuchadnezzar.)

'The young lions do lack and suffer hunger: but they that seek the Lord shall not want any good thing.' (Psalm 34:10)

This particular verse speaks of literal lions being hungry.

Without a single mark being inflicted upon the body, the wounds inflicted from two-legged lions are psychologically painful because they are verbal attacks to the soul. The tongue can become a lethal weapon or be like a spear; it can be sharpened like a sword, a poisonous arrow (bitter words), or a sharp razor through the devising of mischief and deceitfulness.

When the 'lions' found Daniel praying and making his requests known to God, they hastily made audience with King Darius again and reminded him about the fairly new decree, which outlined the penalty for disobedience. They could hardly contain themselves. They accused the innocent Daniel using aggressive language, such as 'That Daniel' (meaning he had no association with them), 'Of the children of the captivity of Judah' (meaning that to them he was a nobody—just a slave, not a satrap), and 'Does not regard you, oh King' (meaning he did not respect King Darius or his laws). They knew that the king had to honour the law, which could not be reversed, and he had to follow the order through.

The Second Lions' Den

In verse 14 of Daniel chapter 6, we hear King Darius's heart of remorse, regret, and repentance. He seems to have understood the motives of the presidents in the end. He was very upset with himself for what he had allowed himself to get involved in at the loss of his servant Daniel. He tried every means possible from sunrise to sunset to undo the damage of the law. Meanwhile, the satraps were probably making grand plans to have a party to mark Daniel's riddance.

With a heavy heart, King Darius commanded that his servant Daniel be placed in the den of lions. He ratified the decree with great reluctance by sealing the stone that was placed on the mouth of the den with his own signet ring. The other conspirators gleefully placed their marks on the stone with their signet rings too, thus sealing their own fates. Prior to that, the king made a profound statement: 'Your God, whom you continually serve, he will deliver you!' King Darius realized, to his regret, what he had done, and there was nothing he could do about it.

During the night, King Darius was restless. He wouldn't eat. He couldn't sleep. No type of wine could numb the anguish he felt for Daniel. He refused company. Not even his wife or maidens were enticing enough to wipe away the feelings of regret from his mind. No sweet music could help him forget what he had unintentionally done in aiding in Daniel's demise. What would encourage a heathen king to give up such luxuries? The attractive lifestyle of his devoted servant. All he could do was to embrace the faith of Daniel by exclaiming that his God was able to deliver him from the den of lions.

Whilst the king was frantic and beside himself about his servant's fate, and whilst the two-legged lions were probably revelling in victory, Daniel enjoyed a good night's sleep. Those four-legged lions were turned into gentle pussycats for the evening because an angel of the Lord was stationed in the den with him and had shut the lions' mouths. God put the lions on a strict fast, promising them an even better meal to come. It doesn't seem to matter how many lions were in that den at all. One can only imagine what kind of night Daniel had.

The next day, early in the morning, and with great urgency, the king ran to the den of lions and called with a lamenting voice to Daniel, 'Oh Daniel, servant of the living God, is your God, whom you serve continually, able to deliver you from the lions?' There was a pause. Silence. Then a voice that the king recognized well replied, 'Oh king, live forever. My God has sent his angel and has shut the lions' mouths, and they have not hurt me, for before him innocence was found in me; and also before you, oh king, have I done no harm.'

Imagine the king's delight. Daniel was immediately released from the den, and upon examination they found no bite marks, torn clothes, or any evidence that suggested that he had spent the night in a den filled with lions. King Darius, in his wrath, commanded that his accusers (all the satraps involved in the conspiracy), and their children and wives be thrown into the den of lions as punishment instead. Well, those lions enjoyed a sumptuous meal and had enough food to last them a good week or so.

Deliverance had been secured because Daniel refused to be intimidated by a bunch of jealous, wicked people. He did not allow his relationship with God to flounder because of a law designed to inflate a king's ego.

It really was a good ending for the king and his servant Daniel. Darius learnt some valuable lessons too. He made a new law written to the people, nations, and languages, saying

'that in very dominion of my kingdom men tremble and fear before the God of Daniel: for he is the living God, and steadfast forever, and his kingdom which shall not be destroyed, and his dominion shall be to the end. He delivers and rescues, and he works signs and wonders in heaven and in earth, who has delivered Daniel from the power of the lions (Daniel 6:26–27).

We applaud King Darius's insight to recognize that there is a God who is able to deliver and set free, and that he indeed works signs and wonders in heaven and earth.

Lessons to Be Learnt

There were two lions' den experiences and two similar outcomes; Daniel came out of them both unscathed. The men (the two-legged lions) who tried to catch him out in terms of his relationship with his God lost their lives instead. And in the real den environment, with four-footed, golden-maned lions, Daniel lived instead of being eaten.

There are so many lessons that we can learn from Daniel's life. One of them is his consistency in his relationship with God. He prayed constantly, even when under pressure. He hadn't done anything wrong, but his foes wanted to find an occasion to accuse him of something.

In the world today, many of us will undergo, or may have undergone, a 'lions' den' situation. We can scarcely avoid them, because after all, we are human, and our contact will always be with other people from various walks of life. The closer we are to people, the more exposed we become to their personalities, characteristics, and mannerisms. If they are pretentious, then it is just a matter of time until their behaviour will eventually reveal their true identities.

Your 'den' could be your home, the place in which you work, the school you attend, your university's halls, or even your church. The 'lions' could include your manager or boss at work, or a co-worker. They could be your friends, who may have turned on you for whatever reason. They could include your spouse, your children, or members of your social circle. You will recognize the roar of the lion and the devastation that lies in its path.

I have personally been in a lions' den environment. It can be a lonely path to walk, and it feels as though the whole world is against you. There were moments when I cried to the Lord in the secret place, with all my emotions raw and muddled, trying to make sense of the dilemmas I faced. But through it all, I pressed on with the emotional strength that he gave me to overcome my trials, and I came out stronger.

In Roman history, the term 'being thrown to the lions' was literally enacted when the early New Testament Christians, who refused to recant their faith in Jesus Christ, were assembled together, tied up in the auditorium, and fed to the lions. I want to encourage you that though the lions may surround you, the Lord promises that he will protect your soul from utter destruction and will deal with the lions accordingly.

In everything we are to give thanks, for this is the will of God in Christ Jesus concerning you (1 Thessalonians 5:18).

'Let your light shine before men, that they may see your good works and glorify your Father which is in heaven' (Matthew 5:16). At the end of the day, this is not about people-pleasing; it is about pleasing the Lord, who delights in righteousness, loving-kindness, and judgement.

Beloved, count it all as joy when you encounter different temptations (James 1:2), like the three Hebrew boys. They did not bow under pressure or run away. They allowed God to decide the outcome of their fate—whether it was to be life or death. There are rewards awaiting all those who suffer for the cause and sake of the name of Jesus Christ.

In Proverbs 6:16–19, Solomon lists the top seven acts that God 'hates': 'A proud look, a lying tongue, and hands that shed innocent blood, An heart that devises wicked imaginations, feet that are swift in running to mischief, A false witness that speaks lies, and he that sows discord among brethren.'

We must surrender our flesh, body, soul, and spirit to God so the Holy Spirit can take mastery over them. In the verses above, the members of the body—the tongue, the hands, the eyes, the feet, and the heart—are guilty of harming another individual, just as in the case of Daniel. These men were conversely guilty of allowing their members to sin against an innocent man. And for that, those two-legged lions were rightly destroyed.

When you are experiencing your lions' den situation, feeling a gamut of emotions, place the problem in the hands of the Master, Jesus. Fighting back is futile, especially when the issue involves more than one person against you. Like Daniel, pour your heart out unto the Lord; he will hear your cries and be your salvation. Whether you are in the throes of a messy divorce, a difficult relationship, or social worries, God will come to your defence; help you to pick up those broken pieces, and make you whole again, healing your soul. He is the balm of Gilead.

There is another lion who is the enemy of our souls. We are reminded in scripture to 'Be sober, be vigilant; because your adversary, the devil, as a roaring lion, walks about seeking whom he may devour' (1 Peter 5:8). But we have a Lion from the Tribe of Judah. He is the King of Kings, and the Lord of all Lords. His name is Jesus, and he can break every chain. He roars against injustice, and he lives forever. He will give us the victory again and again. Hallelujah.

DETERMINING THE VOICE OF GOD
(Based on 1 Samuel 1, 2, and 3)

Samuel's Background

THE TWO COMBINED BOOKS of Samuel tells us about the life of a man who became one of the most recognisable prophets in Old Testament biblical history. We are told how his mother Hannah, begged God to give her a son whom she would dedicate unto the Lord. Samuel's name actually means, 'God has heard', and he was born in answer to her continual prayers of supplication. His early years began in the temple, and from there his prophetic ministry spread throughout Israel - from Dan to Beersheba. His ability to hear from God enabled him to warn and exhort the nation of Israel, and to anoint kings such as Saul and David.

Hannah's prayer to the Lord was punctuated by tears, sincerity, and a promise. Her greatest request was that God would grant her just one male child. Every year when Elkanah and his family went up to Shiloh to offer up their sacrifices, Hannah made it her duty to be in the house of God to pour out her request to get pregnant and have a child.

Penninah, who was the other wife of Elkanah, constantly provoked Hannah both because she had no children of her own and also because Penninah had children from the same husband, whom they shared.

Sometimes nothing inspires motivation like provocation. Hannah didn't retaliate. Instead she sought the face of God with supplications, prayers, and promises. One day whilst in the temple, in the bitterness of her soul, she poured out her heart to him. She promised the Lord that if he granted her a child, she would

1. Give the child back to the Lord for the rest of his life,
2. not allow a razor to touch his hair, and
3. raise him as be a Nazarene child, set apart and holy unto the Lord (see Judges 13:7 and Numbers 6:1–21).

As she wept, Eli the priest sat upon a seat by a post of the temple of the Lord. And it came to pass, as she continued praying before the Lord, that Eli marked her mouth' (1 Samuel 1:9, 12).

Hannah spoke in her heart; only her lips moved, but her voice was not heard: so Eli thought she had been drunken. (1 Samuel 1:13).

And Eli said to her, How long will you be drunk? Put away your wine from you. Eli had incorrectly judged her. She explained her plight to him and added, 'Count not your handmaid for a daughter of Belial: for out of the abundance of my complaint and grief I have spoken'. Then Eli answered and said, 'Go in peace: and the God of Israel grant you your request that you have asked of him' (1 Samuel 1:14:16-17).

Notice that Elkanah was the 'priest' in the home—the head who led his family into worship. So often it is the other way round, and it is the wives who generally leave the husbands behind. The question must be asked, Why are most men today so disinterested in Christianity, church fellowship, and knowing Christ?

Arguably, there would be sufficient responses to fill an entire book. However, it has been said that when the man goes to church, the whole family follows. But if only the wife and kids go, it leaves an incomplete circle.

When Moses was given the general laws and the Ten

Commandments, amongst them was a mandatory instruction with regard to worship and sacrifice.

'Three times a year you shall keep a feast to me. You shall keep the Feast of Unleavened bread; seven days you shall eat unleavened bread as I commanded you, at the time appointed in the month of Abib, for in it you came out of Egypt. None shall appear before me empty-handed. And the feast of harvest, the first-fruits of your labours, which you have sown in the field: and the feast of the Ingathering, which is in the end of the year, when you have gathered in your labours out of the field. Three times in the year all your males shall appear before the Lord' (Exodus 23:14–17).

What am I stressing here? It would appear that whenever Elkanah's family came up to worship at Shiloh, Penninah's sons would also approach the priest with something in their hands. Knowing that Hannah had no children made Penninah's behaviour towards her insensitive and cruel. The stigma of barrenness was too much for Hannah to bear, especially when she viewed her adversary becoming pregnant multiple times in the family home and successfully having children from the same spouse.

The intensity of shame and humiliation placed on Hannah, who didn't seem to fight Penninah back with words, must have been tremendous. But she cried unto the Lord instead. Her husband was kind and enquired why she cried and had not eaten. He said to her, 'Am I not better to you than 10 sons?' (1 Samuel 1:8). Clearly, he loved her, but it didn't remove the longing she had to have children from her own womb.

At each of these significant events, all the male boys were to be present in the temple. Leviticus 26 has a more detailed account of what they were to bring. In verse 12 of the same chapter, the boys were to bring a handful of wheat to the priest, who was to wave it before the Lord the following day. A blemish-free lamb accompanied this.

Samuel's father, Elkanah, was of Levite descent, and from a family of men who lived in Ephraim, which was not too far from Bethlehem or Jerusalem. Hannah eventually birthed her son through her supplications before God in the temple. Based upon the requirement that she would loan Samuel back to God, she fulfilled her side of the bargain. God repaid her with additional children: three boys and two girls.

How generous and lavish is our Father in heaven. She prayed for one and received six. Her faith is a shining example of what can happen when we delight ourselves in the Lord and commit our ways to him. You can be sure that when we 'lend' to the Lord, he will reward us substantially.

There are many other examples too. In Samuel 1:24, Hannah honours her word by presenting her son to God, by fulfilling the requirement that all males were to be present in the Lord's house and not appear empty-handed.

When the Lord visited her and opened her womb, she gave a prayer of praise similar to the Magnificat given by Mary when the angel Gabriel announced that she would bear the baby Jesus. After Hannah had weaned her son, she was able to present him to Eli and announce that she was the woman he had seen praying with her lips moving, making petition unto the Lord for a son.

And as a gesture of thanksgiving and praise for what the Lord had done for her, she also sent up three bullocks, an ephah of flour, and a bottle of wine.

Chapter 2 informs us in verse 11 that Samuel served God before Eli, the priest, wearing a linen ephod, which was generally reserved for the priesthood of Levites aged from twenty years upwards. Samuel was the youngest ever person in the priesthood, growing up and maturing before the Lord in-house, serving him.

What is most intriguing is that although Hannah saw him only once a year during the special festivities with a new coat for him, he didn't seem clingy or to need to go home because of boredom, tiredness, restlessness, or missing his parents, siblings, or the trappings of everyday life. He seemed to enjoy and relish the presence of the Lord, given the fact that most children of his age would be more interested in making friends with their peers, playing around and socializing, getting an education, and so forth.

In verses 18, 20, and 26 of the same chapter, the words '… he ministered before the Lord' are stressed. He grew before the Lord not just in stature but also in emotional maturity. This refers not just to physical gestures but also to living a consecrated life of service through obedience and sacrifice. His being dressed in a linen ephod means that, despite his age, he was involved in the daily preparations of the temple.

As a miniature lad under the Nazarene vow, he would ensure that light was always available in the temple, which represented Christ as natural light and truth, offering thanksgiving and praise on the altar of incense, where prayer was seen as a fragrant aroma to God. Cleansing in the laver of brass immediately followed prior to service. He would have placed the shewbread on the table as a constant reminder of the close fellowship and communion with God. All these acts were in themselves symbolic of God's presence in a believer's life that is solely given unto sanctification and holiness unto the Lord.

Eli, in a sense, represented Samuel's spiritual father and mentor. Though he had his own faults and did not adequately instruct his own children or discipline them for their rebellion, Eli was still able to mould and shape this young little boy by careful direction and teaching him the fear of the Lord during his time in the temple. (See 1 Samuel 2:22–25). Under Eli's tutelage, Samuel would discover the deeper levels of knowing God more intimately.

One night as Eli and Samuel lay down to sleep, God called Samuel's name, and he naturally got up and ran to Eli.

Let us take a closer look at what we can learn from Samuel's response to hearing from God, and how we can apply it today in our everyday lives.

1. **God's voice will be distinctive and clear.** We don't know how far away Eli was from Samuel in the sleeping quarters, but we do know that Samuel ran to him. It took Eli three massive hints to realize that God was trying to make contact with Samuel and not Eli this time.

In 1 Kings 19:9–13, God spoke to Elijah in a still small voice. This did not happen with noise, theatrics, or fireworks; it was a voice of reason, peace, and acceptance. The closer we get to God, then the clearer and more direct our communion and conversations will be. The devil will seek to usurp the interaction, but we must persistently pursue our relationship with our Father.

2. **Eli equipped Samuel with the right response.** Although Samuel had a biological father, he was at home and was unavailable to provide him with the resources immediately required to get to the next level of his ministry. Psalm 27:10 says, 'When my father and my mother forsake me, then the Lord will take me up.' His heavenly Father was God, and his spiritual father and mentor was Eli. This was the same Eli who was once instrumental in his role as high priest and mediator between God and his people, Israel. Now he was to begin to prepare and equip Samuel for a new ministry— speaking on God's behalf.

Samuel, so young, innocent, and pliable, had been obedient in God's eyes in duty and towards authority. With regard to doing what he was told to do when ministering before the Lord, he demonstrated faithfulness, loyalty, and consistency in his responsibilities. He didn't give up; nor did he complain. But he was prompt in service, whether he was lighting the candlestick, laying out the shewbread, or cleaning the anointed utensils.

Although Samuel was young and inexperienced, he was ready for the next level. Being in the Lord's presence daily didn't do him any harm. It was as though God kept him in a special kind of way, which made his heart tender and loyal to serve without seeking to run home to his parents and siblings. He grew sensible and more mature daily.

Every Samuel needs an Eli, meaning an experienced, seasoned man of God who can speak words of life and encouragement, passing on words of wisdom. We require people of experience who are willing to pass on the baton to the next generation.

In the book of Titus 2:1–2, Paul encourages the young pastor Titus to 'Speak the things which become sound (undisputable) doctrine, by encouraging the aged men to be sober, vigilant, determined, self-controlled, sound in faith love and patience.'

Samuels are to be taught and led by example. They need to see the guidelines heard in order to appropriate them. Verse 7 says, 'In all things showing yourself an example of good works, showing seriousness, thoughtfulness, honest and unspotted.

3. **The words of God are consistent and won't fall to the ground.** Isaiah 55:10–11 says, 'As the rain comes down, and the snow from heaven … so shall my word be that comes out of my mouth; it shall not return to me void, but it shall accomplish that which I please, and it shall prosper in the thing whereto I send it.'

Interestingly, God chose to tell Samuel a piece of information he had previously revealed to Eli through another prophet (1 Samuel 2:27–26). It was less detailed but nonetheless outlined God's displeasure against Eli and his sons. It was a confirmation of what he had said, and it foretold of events to come. It was also a private and personal insight of Eli, and an event that all Israel would be made fully aware of. (See verse 34.)

4. **Sometimes the information contains truths too painful to digest.** The insights that young Samuel received from God made him too afraid and uncomfortable to repeat them to Eli. Imagine being given sensitive information about someone you've grown to have a deep respect for and served. Samuel sensibly kept his mouth shut out of fear and because the

revelation was embarrassing, and he spoke about his spiritual mentor Eli with God. Eli was obviously curious about what God had revealed to Samuel, and he used intimidating language to prise the truth out of him. He said almost threateningly, 'God will do so to you if you hide the words of all the things he told you.'

5. **When you speak God's Word truthfully, the outcome is unpredictable (depending on the recipient!)** The true prophets of God were always subject to reproach, scorn, punishment, killings, and exile. (See Jeremiah, Elisha, Elijah, John the Baptist, Amos, and other examples.) The recipients' attitudes towards truth will also vary. They will either accept or reject it.

Like Samuel, speak the word whether they will hear it or forebear it (Ezekiel chapter 2:7). This was a test that Samuel passed. He spoke, holding nothing back. It must've been very uncomfortable for him do so initially, being so young. But from then on, he was regarded as a well-known and respected prophet in Israel. His words never fell to the ground, and he was always available to hear from God.

May God grant us a Samuel-like antenna that will seek to tune into his wavelength for such a time as this.

DIVIDED LOYALTIES: WHOSE SIDE ARE YOU ON?
(Based on the Story of Sheba and Amasa, 2 Samuel 20)

PRINCE ABSALOM WAS DEAD, and his father, King David, mourned bitterly for him. Whilst he was still alive, he revolted against the king with cruel ambition. To make matters even worse, he removed Joab from his prestigious post as captain and instead promoted Amasa in his place, who was now his new supporter.

Amasa was David's nephew through Zeruiah, his sister, and he was Joab's cousin. So he probably revelled in the knowledge that he was siding with his uncle's son, Absalom, in his position as captain of the host. However, after Absalom's demise, Amasa was now between a rock and a hard place because he had initially deserted King David.

Joab spoke strong words of advice to David during his bereavement when he said the following:

'You have embarrassed the faces of all your servants today, and the lives of your sons and daughters, and the lives your wives and concubines; In that you love your enemies, and hated your friends, for you have declared this day, that you regard neither princes nor servants: for this day I know, that if Absalom had lived, and all we had died this day, then it had pleased you well. Now therefore arise, and go forth, and speak comfortably unto your servants: for I swear by the Lord, if you don't go forth, there will not tarry one with you this night: and that will be worse unto you than all the evil that befell you from your youth till now' (2 Samuel 19:5-7).

Powerful words indeed from a man who had just murdered the very son he was meant to protect and keep alive!

Shamefully, the people had quickly united with David's son, and as soon as they realized that he was dead, they fled back into their tents in terror and fear because the king was back. In verse 9 of 2 Samuel 19, the people responded by saying,

The king saved us out of the hand of our enemies, and he delivered us out of the hand of the Philistines; and now he has fled out of the hand of Absalom. And Absalom, whom we anointed over us, is dead in battle. Now then why did you not speak a word of bringing the king back? Now David was in Jerusalem, and he addressed the people at the gate.

Once David had spoken to Zadok and Abiathar, the priests, who were to speak to the elders of Judah, he then had to explain and tell the people in love,

'You are my brethren, you are my bones and my flesh?' David then went on to say to Amasa, 'Are you not of my bone and of my flesh: God to so to me, and more if you be not captain of the host before me continually instead of Joab' (2 Samuel 19:12-13).

David spoke kindly towards the people and acknowledged them so they would feel accepted and comfortable around him again. He desired no harm to come upon them, considering that their loyalty towards him was so inconsistent. One moment they sided with Absalom, and then they sided with Sheba.

Amasa had now received a second promotion: one had come earlier from Absalom and the other was from David, his uncle. Meanwhile, Joab received a double demotion—one demotion from Absalom, for Amasa (2 Samuel 17:25), and the other from David for Amasa (2 Samuel 19:13).

So although Joab had diplomatically contrived to reconcile David to Absalom with the widow of Tekoa by killing him, he had placed himself on the radar of David, who had been informed about what Joab had done against his wishes.

David showed mercy to Amasa in that instant, even though Amasa had been so quick and foolish to follow someone else twice. He also extended immediate mercy to Joab by not exacting instantaneous death for killing his son, leaving that obligation to be executed by his son Solomon when he was on his deathbed.

When it looked like everything was calm and peaceful, another problem was brewing elsewhere. There was an incident whereby a man called Sheba decided to challenge David's royal leadership position. Not only was he the son of Bichri, but he was also a man of Belial. (His name, Sheba, means 'oath'.) This happened not too long after David was restored in Jerusalem after the death of his son, who also had sought to take the kingdom by force. Sheba was probably aware of this, and one must wonder what on earth was going on in his mind for him to want to destroy and usurp the king.

One day, he blew a trumpet and said in an audible voice,

'We have no part in David, neither have we inheritance in the son of Jesse: every man to his tents, Oh Israel'. So every man of Israel went up from after David, and followed Sheba the son of Bichri: but the men of Judah clave unto their king, from Jordan even to Jerusalem' (2 Samuel 20:1-2).

Sheba was clearly disgruntled about something and had most likely been planning for days, weeks, or even months what he would say and do, and when he would say or do it. He might have been angry about the fact that when David returned to Jerusalem, it was the tribe of Judah that conducted him safely over from the River Jordan, and also half the people of Israel. A heated argument broke out between the tribe of Judah and the remaining tribes of Israel.

The people of Israel came to the king and said,

Why have our brethren (Judah) stolen you away, and have brought the king and his men with him over Jordan? The men of Judah replied, because the king is near of kin to us: why then are you angry for this matter? Have we eaten at all of the king's cost? Or has he given us a gift? (2 Samuel 19:42)

The men of Israel said to the men of Judah, 'We have 10 parts in the king, and we have also more right in David than you: why did you despise us that our advice should not be first in bringing back our king? (2 Samuel 19:43)

It was a fierce debate exacerbated by Israel but strongly fought by Judah.

This is the opening backdrop to the second revolt that King David experienced, but this time the revolt came from the lawless man Sheba. Interestingly, this man needed some important people to consolidate with him in his deluded quest for fame, recognition, and power.

Sheba, a man of Belial, was classed as a wicked and worthless individual with two fathers: a biological one and a demonic one—a son of Belial. He was a troublemaker who no doubt had no trouble manipulating the people's emotions enough to speak on their behalf and have them follow his instructions. After just one short announcement, these people—who should have learned their lesson from the previous attempt by Absalom—went back to their tents at the command of this upstart.

In verse 2, we are awed by the loving loyalty and generous support of the tribe of Judah, who supported David and believed in his authority. God will always have someone to help and support you in your struggles. David was looking to God to sustain him through this incredible dilemma. He was just coming to terms with his bereavement over his son Absalom, and now this evil person was creating havoc in his monarchy through evil communications. In fact, as a result of this, the people began to cling to Sheba as an authority figure.

As before, David refused to touch the Lord's anointed. Even though Sheba was in no shape or form anointed, David left vengeance to God. He recognized that with his dealings with Bathsheba and Uriah, he was truly forgiven, but the consequences of it came at a heavy cost that started from within his home.

In verse 4, David summoned his newly appointed commander-in-chief, Amasa, to assemble the men of Judah and report back within three days. 'So Amasa went to assemble to the men of Judah: but he tarried longer than the set time which he [David] had appointed him.'

Amasa, whose name means 'burden', was a very fickle character. One never knew whose side he was on. He proved himself unfaithful when he happily unhinged himself from his initial loyalty to David in order to support Absalom, who then quickly promoted him as leader of the army. Now it appeared that Sheba had also called for his help, and he readily sided with him too. On these two occasions, he switched his loyalties, and he had proven to be a very dangerous agent. As he was a chief leader over David's army, that could lead to all sorts of mischief.

What was Amasa's gripe, one may ask?

Maybe he secretly feared that David's kingdom was in for another hammering. Maybe he had heard through his strong connections that a ruse was being planned against David and he wanted to escape whilst the opportunity was available.

When he failed to appear within the days requested, David said to Abishai,

'Now shall Sheba the son of Bichri do us more harm than did Absalom: Take your lords' servants, and chase after them otherwise he'll get the fenced cities.' And there went out after him Joab's men, and the Chereithites, and the Pelethites and all the mighty men: and they went out of Jerusalem to chase after Sheba the son of Bichri' (vv. 6–7).

Abishai was one of the most trusted mighty men of the host, and straightaway they went out to capture and kill the conspirator Sheba. Again, it's interesting to note here that David sent them out against Sheba, not Amasa. Why? Could it be that his tender protective heart leaned towards his disloyal nephew? Did he instinctively know within himself that Amasa had possibly been coerced into teaming up with Sheba?

Joab, on the other hand, had a grudge that needed fixing. He had heard the officers say 'chase after' Sheba, but in his head he had heard 'kill Amasa and kill Sheba'. Joab, the Destroyer, had a job to fulfil, and he would not rest until it was done. Amasa had done an injustice to the king who had favoured him and promoted him

36

within the army's ranks, and now he was joining himself wholly to this unsavoury fellow.

Joab and his mighty men finally caught up with Amasa at a great stone in Gibeon. With a show of feigned affability, he greeted him and said,

'Are you in good health, my brother?' And Joab took Amasa by the beard with the right hand to kiss him. Amasa paid no attention to the sword that had dropped prior to their encounter ... so (Joab) smote him with the sword in the fifth rib, and shed out his bowels to the ground, and struck him not again; and he died. Then he left him and along with his brother Abishai they chased after Sheba the son of Bichri' (2 Samuel 20:9).

What a gruesome and brutal way to die! Joab had exacted his fury and vengeance on a man who kept swapping his allegiances with people—first with King David, then with Absalom, and now with Sheba. By doing so, he was dishonouring the king and exposing the king to danger by joining forces with the aforementioned individuals, which in Joab's eyes was unacceptable and amounted to treason. Secondly, he was promoted over Joab as head of the army on two occasions, which would have infuriated him. Joab was not his friend, but in order to get near to him, he had to appear friendly. 'Faithful are the wounds of the friends, but the kisses of the enemy are deceitful' (Proverbs 27:6).

In verse 12 of chapter 20, we are told that '... Amasa wallowed in blood in the midst of the highway. And when the man saw that all the people stood still, he removed Amasa out of the highway into the field, and cast a cloth upon him, when he saw that everyone that came by him stood still.' That was the best 'burial' they could do for him.

Graphically, it was not a pretty sight; Amasa was disembowelled and bloodied. The consequences for sin are always harrowing, no matter how trivial the offence. Amasa, had betrayed David twice by running away to another man who lacked a sense of justice and moral substance. That was the price he paid for treachery towards the king and the assault to Joab's pride. God always has a man or woman reserved to defend the causes of those who put their trust in Him.

Now they were on the move to eliminate Sheba once and for all. He was a wanted man, and now the whole country was gathered, out to get him. Following him in hot pursuit, Joab went throughout the tribes and collected people on the way from Abel-Bethmaachah, which was situated in northern Palestine.

The day was long, and as they approached the city where Sheba was hiding, the people with Joab besieged the city by battering the wall to cast it down. Joab was prepared to destroy the city for the sake of that one man. But a woman, in her wisdom, caught his attention, as recorded in verse 16.

'Come here that I may speak with you.' She asked him, 'Are you Joab?' To which he replied, 'I am he.' Listen to the words of your handmaid. (When you read the story of the widow of Tekoa, you realise that Joab has a soft spot for wise old women). In olden time, they used to say, They shall surely ask counsel at Abel: and so they ended the matter. I am one of them that are peaceable and faithful in Israel: you seek to destroy a city and a mother in Israel: why will you swallow up the inheritance of the Lord?

Joab tactfully and respectfully answered the woman with this reply:

'Far be it, far be it from me, that I should swallow up and destroy. That is not the case: but a man of mount Ephraim, Sheba the son of Bichri has lifted up his hand against the king, even against David: deliver him only, and I will leave the city. The woman said, 'Behold, his head shall be thrown to thee over the wall.' Then the woman in her wisdom, went unto all the people and they cut off the head of Sheba, and threw it out to Joab. And he blew a trumpet, and they retired from the city, and every man returned home. And Joab returned to Jerusalem unto the king' (2 Samuel 20:20-22).

The twenty-third verse shows how he was reinstated to his normal office as commander-in-chief over the house of Israel. He would have had to declare that David's nephew Amasa was killed, and he was probably not too forthcoming with the details of his death. However, David called it to account at the end of his days. We do not get an inkling of David's feelings regarding the death of Amasa, his relative, or even Sheba, but at least they no longer posed a threat to his kingdom.

Lessons We Can Learn from This Story

In this story, David represents King Jesus, whom we are supposed to remain loyal and constant to for myriad reasons. As king, David provided for the needs of the nation that he served. In this story, we discover the many twists and turns of individuals who turned up their heels against him and betrayed him.

Sheba symbolizes the rebellious and reckless individuals that society is filled with today. Although under the leadership of the king, he decided to start a revolution and take others along with him in his quest to undermine the one God had personally chosen. Amasa represents the weak-willed individual who follows with blind allegiance, to his own peril.

Jesus has done all he can to make our lives comfortable here on earth with all its woes. There will be people like the tribe of Judah and the bodyguards, who will remain steadfast and reliable to the end. On the other hand, there will be people who may initially support you and have your back, only to later dismiss you altogether. Jesus also experienced disloyalty and betrayal amongst his disciples in the form of Judas, who plotted with the high priests for financial gain. The story didn't end well for him!

Nevertheless, Jesus remains the same, and he will always be loyal to us unconditionally as we stay with him, loving and respecting his laws and instructions. He promises that he'll see us through even when we fall seven times along life's journey, even in our darkest hours (Isaiah 43:1, Psalm 27:1).

As children of God, we are living in the last days, like Noah. The world has turned its back on their Creator and, like sheep, has gone astray. Jesus will divide the world into two camps, and many shall surrender their lives to him. But many shall unfortunately deny him, and there shall be a great falling away.

When it comes to divided loyalties, no man can serve two masters at the same time, as there will be a tug of affections over time if he does so. Matthew 6:24 cautions us that 'One will hate the one master and love the other, or hold to one and despise the other.'

We cannot serve God and Mammon. Jesus said that 'it is hard for them that trust in riches to enter the kingdom of God; but with him all things are possible' (Mark 10:24, 27).

Joshua, in his final exhortation with the children of Israel, said, 'Choose today whom you will serve; whether the gods which your fathers served ... but as for me and house we will serve the Lord' (Joshua 24:15).

In society today, when we are given the opportunity to vote for a potential MP candidate to serve within his or her local constituency, we are given a slip of paper with a few names listed. We may have an idea of who the candidates are from the press, articles in the tabloids, or other media outlets. When attending the polling station, a voter's identity is checked against another list to ensure that he or she is eligible to vote. Then the voter is shown to a booth to mark an X on the paper privately. That paper is then folded in half and placed inside a large box, which will later be opened, and the votes counted. In this case, the person has the option to either reject, accept, or 'spoil' the voting paper. Although thousands of people choose their ideal candidates, their loyalties are divided in various ways because of the power of free will.

When it comes to the kingdom of God, there will be no sitting on the fence. It will either be yes or no to God, or yes or no to Satan. The fight is over our souls, and the choices we make will ultimately determine our destinies.

Our loyalties to God will cost us not financially but with our lives. Timothy said that 'if we suffer for him, we shall also reign with him' (2 Timothy 2:12). Paul said that 'if we endure to the end, the same shall be saved' (Romans 10:13). John the Revelator said, 'Blessed are they that do his commandments, that they may have right to the tree of life and may enter in through the gates into the city' (Revelation 22:14).

We are either the children of light or the children of darkness. We either love the world and serve Satan or love the Father and serve Him. We are either a new creature and walk in the Spirit or we walk according to the flesh under the old Adamic nature and continue in sin that grace may abound. We either are on the broad way or pass through the narrow gate that leads to life. We are classed as either the five wise virgins or the five foolish virgins.

May we stay loyal, faithful, dedicated, and steadfast to Him who is the Author and Finisher of our faith—the Alpha and Omega, the First and the Last. He is our Rear Guard and the great Rewarder of them that diligently seek him. He that promised is faithful and will pay every man, woman, boy, and girl as their work dictates.

In the story of Sheba and Amasa, these individuals both met awful deaths because of their disloyalty towards King David. People will die for not accepting Jesus as King, and for the penalty he paid, in order for them to receive immortality in his eternal kingdom.

May this cautionary tale propel us to hold unswerving loyalty towards God. In the words of Jesus, 'When I come back, will I find faith on earth?' (Luke 18:8).

DOOMED REVELATIONS
(Based on Isaiah Chapter 39)

IN THE PROPHETIC BOOK of the prophet Isaiah, chapter 39, we are brought face to face with three main characters: Hezekiah, Merodach-baladan, and Isaiah.

Hezekiah was a righteous king who sought to please and keep the commandments of the Lord. During his reign, he received threats from King Sennacherib, who was a cruel and evil individual. This treacherous king ruled Assyria in 701BC and invaded Judah whilst 'caging up' Hezekiah in the city of Jerusalem.

During his campaign, he also pilfered forty-six cities and took two hundred thousand captives alive. Hezekiah's relationship with Sennacherib and Merodach-baladan would have doubtless been quite strained, to say the least.

Hezekiah also underwent a period of ill-health, which turned out to be terminal. Based on verse 1 of the same chapter, he was sick unto death. Through the prophet Isaiah, he received instructions from the Lord to prepare himself to die; to organize his will and effects. It would appear that he did not take this message too well, because he wept bitterly before God, with his face turned towards the wall. He reminded God of his stellar, dutiful service and how he had lived righteously all his life.

God could not fault him on such an outstanding track record, and in his mercy, God granted him (1) a sign of the sun going down by ten degrees and shadow, (2) a cure arrived at by placing the figs on a boil, and (3) extension of life of an additional fifteen years. God is lavish in his mercies.

A record of Hezekiah's prayer and thanksgiving is detailed in Isaiah 38:9–22.

After such a gracious deliverance, Hezekiah received letters and a present from the same Merodach-baladan, son of Baladan, king of Babylon in roughly 705 BC. He was made aware of Hezekiah's sickness and recovery.

In verse 2 of the brief chapter 39, there is a sense that Hezekiah was very happy for the gift or gifts that the men gave to him, and he duly took Merodach-baladan and the delegates, the princes of Babylon, and showed them *everything* that he had amassed in his lifetime.

In the past, when God had marvellously delivered him from out the hand of Sennacherib with the inhabitants of Jerusalem, he had made him extremely wealthy. Many nations had heard about his fame and also brought gifts to him, and he was magnified and made famous amongst the nations from that time onwards.

Hezekiah left no stone unturned in showing the visitors what he had. He was extremely wealthy, so much so that he made himself treasuries (or storehouses) for his silver, gold, precious stones, spices, shields, and jewels. In addition, he had storehouses for corn, wine, and oil; stalls for beasts and flocks; and so forth. All this Hezekiah allowed the foreigners to behold with their eyes in exchange for something: a gift and a letter!

By close examination of this crucial verse, it is understood that Hezekiah didn't seem to give credit to God for his recovery or advise the dignitaries that the Lord can give people success when they put him first. There is no mention of this anywhere. However, it is noted that absolutely *everything* was shown of his wealth, prestige, and substance! 'If riches increase, set not your heart upon them!' (Psalm 62:10).

Verse 3 introduces us to the prophet Isaiah confronting Hezekiah with just three questions:

1. What did the men say?
2. Where did they come from?

3. What have they seen in your house?

These questions deserve thorough scrutiny, don't they? After all, we can detect something much deeper rumbling under the surface when we explore the nature of these probing questions which were meant to provoke Hezekiah's own thoughts and intentions.

What did the men say? These men travelled from afar to congratulate Hezekiah on his health, but did they actually come to make war or peace? What was the intention behind their visit? What was written in the letter? Was it lengthy? Who was the letter from? Was it brief or detailed? What did they ask of Hezekiah? What did they want to know? Were they asking for assistance with taxes, policies, or kingdom-related issues? Did they say anything that would make Hezekiah doubt their motives for visiting him? What present did they give Hezekiah? Was the gift something he could use in the military? Was the gift something he could put up in the courtroom or courtyard, or the palace? Unfortunately, Isaiah received no answer when he asked what the men said.

Where did they come from? Hezekiah was able to answer this one. This question was easy. In fact, it was too easy. He answered the question honestly, but with an element of pride. 'They came from a far country (to me), even from Babylon' (Isaiah 39:3). Hezekiah didn't seem to register what he had done. The visit seemed innocent enough. After all, these important foreign neighbours visited him with a gift, so as a kind of gesture and with open arms, he accepted them into his palace and gave them a free grand tour. Babylon was a place associated with idolatry, corruption, and hostility; and it was an enemy of Israel who had captured them many times, and now these guys were his buddies?

What had they seen in his house? This was another important question that was far too easy to reply to. Hezekiah didn't even stop to consider the implications of his actions. Nor did he pause to think why in the world Isaiah would ask him such simple questions or ponder the meaning of their importance. His response signified pride.

One other point worth mentioning is the number of times he referred to himself: 'They have seen everything', '... nothing left unseen.' In his response to Isaiah he states, '... in my house', '... my treasures', and '... I have shown' (Isaiah 39:4).

What was also intriguing was that the princes didn't reveal anything about their military strategies, plans, or ideas. When Isaiah asked Hezekiah, 'What did they say', he didn't have an answer for it.

This king was drunk with success, and pride flowed through his veins during this opportunity to show off to his enemies what he had accumulated. Hezekiah's actions were rash, vain, and foolish. He should have acted with caution.

It was only afterwards that Isaiah dropped the bombshell. He stated that the Lord said a time was coming soon when all that Hezekiah had amassed, would be taken away to Babylon; nothing would remain. Even his very children would be taken from him, and they would stand before the king of Babylon as captive eunuchs. This was fulfilled in the book of Daniel, where Daniel himself was a captive and was made a eunuch in the land of Babylon, alongside Hananiah, Mishael, and Azariah (later Shadrach, Meschech, and Abednego).

Also interesting was that God didn't give any reasons why he would do this. It seemed as though it was left up to Hezekiah to figure it out for himself or to ask God via Isaiah. But sadly, we see that he did not; rather, he passively resigned to his fate. In 2 Chronicles 32, we are told that God left him to his devices to see what was in his heart.

What lessons can we learn from chapter 39 regarding Hezekiah? There are quite a few.

- Once Hezekiah recovered from his sickness, he failed to give glory to God. Instead he used his energies in providing insider information to a distant enemy, Babylon.
- It would seem apparent that Merodach-baladan was trying to curry favour with Hezekiah, having been made aware of his triumphs and victories over his conquests, and the wealth he had accumulated. The gift in question was a form of

gesture that Hezekiah was naturally accustomed to, but he should've been more wary than to give the princes a grand tour in return.

- When God has done something wonderful in our lives, we must give him the praise and thanksgiving due to him, as a living sacrifice. This would have been a great opportunity for Hezekiah to tell the princes what God had done for him.
- Be careful whom you take your gifts from! 'A gift blinds the eyes of the wise, and perverts (distorts) the words of the righteous' (Exodus 23:8). These men had ulterior motives and had Hezekiah spotted it, his sons would not have ended up in Babylon as captives far from home.

The houses were filled with the following:

Silver	Ointments (aromatic)	Storehouses
Gold	Shields	Stalls
Spices (aromatic powders)	Treasures	Flocks, herds, horses

This could represent our lives. The book of Proverbs states, 'Keep (guard) your heart with all carefulness, for out of it are the issues (matters) of life' (Proverbs 4:23).

The silver and gold represent the precious core values and principles that you uphold and treasure and cherish as most important to you in your life, including your personhood, marriage, family, assets, collections you may pass on to next generation, heirlooms, family photos, albums, memories, children, career, home, financial security, friends, loyalty, respect, and ethics.

The ointment and spices represent things of worth that also contain valuable benefits due to their uniqueness, such as time, life skills such as being an artist, cook, doctor, surgeon, making jewellery, engineer, musician, and potter, etc, and commitment—special and precious things that should not be sold.

The shields represent boundaries: personal boundaries, family boundaries, emotional boundaries, and relationship boundaries; and, within your home, protection, security, and equipment to help in the event of an attack.

Corn represents substance, whether financial, material, spiritual, relational, social, or emotional and mental, as well as blessings. It does not just refer to what you eat.

Wine and oil represent the anointing of the Holy Ghost, and thus joy, happiness, and gladness.

The storerooms which held the corn, oil, wine, and so forth could symbolize our thought processes, plans, ideas, dreams, aspirations, ambitions, goodness, and precious treasures.

Our souls are composed of our emotions, dreams, thoughts, aspirations, ideas, wills, desires, and minds. And to part with our souls is not only dangerous but also destructive. We must remember that the enemy may see the things that we possess and plan how to use them to their advantage.

In this instance, Hezekiah failed to recognize his actions in regard to showing off his shields, and he let the enemy in on his military strategies, armoury, plans, and secrets without giving any thought to any future consequences. This is similar to handing over a password to a stranger telling him or her to use it!

Never let your guard down in a situation like this. 'The thief doesn't come just to steal, but to kill and destroy ...' (John 10:10). This is precisely what happened, just as Isaiah had prophesied.

Our lives are precious and special. To allow toxic relationships into our lives is fatal. They will raid your 'house' without your permission, trampling on anything they may regard as worthless (belonging to you) and stealing anything that is of benefit or value to themselves or others.

They may mimic, camouflage, or use tactics to reproach you. Guard your heart, mouth, and life. Learn to possess your vessel in sanctification and honour towards God (1 Thessalonians 4:4).

If we fail to guard our lives' 'houses' from outside attack and we expose secrets about ourselves, we leave ourselves vulnerable to the attack of the adversary. Hezekiah tragically learned that one can have it all and lose everything in an instant, with all of it falling into the wrong hands.

The questions posed to Hezekiah were meant to prompt him to reflect on his behaviour and to realize what he had done. His responses to all three suggest that he assumed he hadn't done anything wrong in his eyes. God was displeased and in return told him that everything he'd exposed would soon be nothing, all of it taken away by the same enemy he had allowed to initially view everything for his and their pleasure.

A good man, out of the good treasure of his heart, brings out good things; and an evil man, out of the evil treasure of his heart, brings forward evil things (Matthew 12:35).

In the case of Hezekiah, he showed many of the treasures God had bestowed on him. In particular, the princes were not shown anything regarding religion or worship, the temple, ordinances, and the like. (It is possible that the scriptures would tell us that if he had.) The foremost reason for their visit was to congratulate Hezekiah on his recovery, which they attributed to their venerable sun god, whom they assumed turned had turned ten degrees backwards as a sign for Hezekiah.

Assyria was an enemy of Babylon because Assyria was in tribute to Babylon, so Baladan saw this as a unique opportunity to join forces with Hezekiah and thus strengthen his side against Babylon.

We are cautioned in this tale not to trade our personal values to foreigners and strangers.

The Babylonians were considered enemies to God's people and had on occasion brought them into captivity. That same nation stripped Hezekiah of every single possession that he owned, including his very children. They eventually became eunuchs in the palace of Babylon. (See Daniel 1).

Today, revealing personal information or secrets to unvetted persons, regardless of their status, can seriously lead one into emotional or psychological slavery, bondage, or servitude to those one reveals such information to.

Let us learn from Hezekiah's life not to be so revealing to enemies and strangers. Doing so can lead to all sorts of trouble!

GOD'S AUCTION ROOM

THERE ARE A FEW shows dedicated to auctioneering, including *Cash in the Attic, Money for Nothing, Bargain Hunt, Flog It*, and *Antiques Roadshow*. People will visit jumble sales, car boot sales, and antique shops, scouring for a valuable item or a good bargain. Furthermore, they might research an item or get an evaluation. Where there has been damage, a person can lovingly restore an item back to good condition or arrange for it to be repaired by specialists who deal in a particular area of expertise so that it can then be sold. The owner may store it away, or he or she may sell it to make a profit.

Sometimes an item may be passed on within the generational family like a precious heirloom. It could be a soldier's medal, a piece of jewellery, a doll, or anything else of value from a deceased individual or perhaps a benefactor. When a valuation is placed on the item, then insurance can be arranged to cover its cost.

A typical auction room consists of an auctioneer with a gavel, keen buyers, hungry sellers, lots (items), bids and bidders, specialists who are experts in their fields of knowledge, and private memorabilia collectors.

There are multiple sections of items that are found in an auction room. You will find jewellery, tables and chairs, pottery, vases, period pieces, historical pieces, paintings, drawings, military paraphernalia, furniture, art, coins, books, stamps, dolls, bears, toys, cards—the list is endless.

Items are initially inspected for wear and tear, and especially for authenticity. Experts will inspect an item and glean its historical background and origin. Defects and chips are noted and are taken into account regarding the item's overall value and price. Originality, age, and condition all count in the eyes and appeal of eager bidders.

An opening bid is made by the auctioneer whilst the product is held aloft and shown to those in the room. The floor is then opened to bids. Those interested can make their interest known by a wave of their hand or sheet, a nod, or a wave of their paddle or numbered card. The keen-eyed auctioneer scans the room quickly to ensure that no one is overlooked. The value of the lot may increase or decrease relative to its starting price, or it may remain unsold, depending on the interest or disinterest of those in the room or on the Internet. Interested bidders make their interest known until they are outbid.

Historical pieces generally attract huge amounts of interest as well as profits, especially if the items belonged to or were made by someone famous. Money passes through hands many times, and a slice of the money made is taken as a commission.

Items may carry defects: scratches, dents, marks, chips, breaks, and apparent repairs. The condition of a piece is important, as is the place of origin, the manufacturer, and the maker of the item. The time period of its creation also adds weight to its value and condition.

Like the items assembled in the auction room, no matter how flawed, unworthy, devalued by society, emotionally dented, chipped, or scratched, Jesus accepts us all based on his character, not ours. It matters not whether you spent years incarcerated in prison, had a traumatic past, or are emotionally scarred; he lovingly waits to receive you and restore you to his original design and the template of our true identity.

No matter the state that we find ourselves in, whether we are indebted, divorced, depressed, miserable, traumatized, or insecure, in God's eyes he sees us as

his workmanship created in him [Christ Jesus] unto good works, which God has before prepared (already ordained) that we should walk in them. (Ephesians 2:10)

There are many people in the Bible who had faults and flawed characters but whom God restored and received—for example:

Rahab, Jacob, Abraham, the children of Israel, David, and King Manasseh, to name but a few.

There are people who accumulate and amass wealth of great earthly value only. On this side of life, it gives people confidence and security that they have assets that are not only liquid. But scripture tells us, 'For what shall it profit a man, if he shall gain the whole world, and lose his own soul? … or what shall a man give in exchange for his soul?' (Mark 8:6, 37). In another passage, we are encouraged to '*lay up our treasures in heaven, where neither moth or rust doesn't corrupt, nor thieves cannot break through or steal*' (Matthew 6:20).

Jesus purchases those who accept his sacrifice based on his precious blood, not with coins: 'For you are bought with a price, so then glorify God in your body and in your spirit which is God's' (1 Corinthians 6:20).

Jeremiah 1:5 says, 'Before I formed you in the belly, I knew you, and before you came out of the womb I sanctified you.'

In Isaiah 61:1, the Lord proclaims through Luke,

The spirit of the Lord is upon me; because the Lord has anointed me to preach good tidings unto the meek; he has sent me to bind up the broken-hearted, to proclaim liberty to the captives, and the opening of the prison to them that are bound whether mentally, emotionally or psychologically crippled.

Some sellers end up taking their items home because there was no interest shown in the products or they couldn't fetch the prices they were valued or reserved at. But Jesus says, 'All that the Father gives me shall come to me; and him that comes to me I will no wise cast out' (John 6:37).

We all have pasts and have suffered traumatic, sordid, scandalous lifestyles. We may have secrets—skeletons in our closets that for some extend to many generations. All of us are in need of a saviour, and that's why Jesus Christ came into the world to fulfil that criteria of saving sinners. If we were able to rip out some of the pages of our lives to reveal a healthier picture of the better parts of ourselves, then indeed we would. But we would not be authentic. God sees us as whole people, warts and all, with our combined successes and failures, and our psychological scars and bruises. But in his eyes, we are still viewed as lovable, redeemable, forgivable, and worthy.

As with the items in an auction room, somebody may see value in something that another person might have missed; and because they know its true cost and appeal, they may be willing to make the purchase and take it away before someone else removes it.

This is much more the case with Jesus, who knows our true value. His blood transforms us and makes us brand new. He repairs our poor self-esteem and works on our flawed character so that we conform to his righteousness by grace. When we sin, we have an advocate—one who stands on our side—because he already tasted sin for all of us, who knew no sin. When we stray off the narrow course, as the Good Shepherd, he knows just how to lead us into right direction and secure our souls. When we are downtrodden, then as the Prince of Peace, he knows how to inject calm and tranquillity within our situations.

It does not matter who you are, where you come from, where you live, or what you are going through. Whether you are male, female, young or old, rich or poor, a boy or a girl, Jesus Christ loves you. You are precious to Him despite the many mistakes you have committed.

What is man that you are mindful of him? And the son of man, that you visit him? (Psalm 8:4)

Your thoughts towards each individual is very precious (Psalm 139:17)

The very hairs on our heads are numbered. (Luke 12:7)

Look, I have graven you upon the palms of my hands; your walls are continually before me. (Isaiah 49:12)

We are not unredeemable. Because God so loved the world, and still loves us, he is not willing for any to perish. Instead we are to have everlasting life. (see John 3:16). So then, regardless of our condition, he will purchase us and restore us back to wholeness with a deep love for his Son. Not only that, but he also gives us the promise of an even better life in the earth made new, in the heavenly kingdom of God.

In God's auction room, everybody matters.

YOUR HOUSE TYPE—
ROCK OR SAND
(Based on Matthew 7:24-27)

I BEGIN MY REFLECTION WITH the story about three little pigs who all lived together under one roof. One day, they had a huge argument and all decided to move out and live independently. So each pig took its belongings, and they found different locations for their new homes.

The first pig decided to build his house from straw. It looked rather impressive until Mr Wolf came along to inspect it. He knocked on the door for a chat.

Wolf: 'May I come in?'

Pig 1: No, you can't!

Wolf: If you don't, I'll huff and I'll puff, and I'll blow your house down!'

Pig 1: 'Well, you just go ahead and try!'

So the wolf huffed and puffed and blew the house of straw down. Pig 1 escaped with his life. The same incident happened to Pig 2, who so happened to build his house from wood. Not long after, the wolf came over to the next pig to pay it a visit. This house also looked good, but after a few huffs and puffs from the wolf, that house also collapsed. The piggy ran and escaped by the skin of his teeth. (These houses couldn't have taken very long to erect given the ease with which the wolf blew them down).

Finally, the third pig was just putting the finishing touches on his house built from brick when the wolf paid him a personal visit with a view to a delicious bacon meal, demanding that they talk inside the house. After some rejection, the wolf began huffing and puffing, and he eventually realized that he was wasting his time with this house, as it was too strong for him to demolish.

In the end, when the other pigs saw the wisdom of the third pig's choice of house, they decided to stop there and live in harmony together again.

This delightful children's story, which I've slightly exaggerated, has something to tell us. The obvious message is that if you spend time building a strong house, then you will be protected from external damage or danger. The pigs symbolize people, whilst the wolf is depicts Satan in disguise. His character traits are always there; they are not always easy to detect, but the signs of deceitful friendliness and enticing words of kindness just serve as a cover for something more sinister. (The pigs hadn't worried about how their houses would stand, thinking they would be fine as long as they had roofs over their heads and the weather was always sunny).

In the parable of Matthew chapter 7:24–27, Jesus tells us about two people.

… Whoever hears these sayings of mine, and does them, I will liken him unto a wise man, which built his house upon a rock: And the rain descended, and the floods came, and the winds blew, and beat upon that house; and it fell not: for it was founded upon a rock. And every one that hears these sayings of mine and does them not, shall be likened unto a foolish man, which built his house upon the sand: And the rain descended, and the floods came, and the winds blew, and beat upon that house; and it fell: and great was the fall of it.

When you are considering building your house, you must first consider the type of soil you will use. The soil must be analysed and meet stringent standards before it can be incorporated. A good foundation is also strongly recommended.

Over the years, houses have literally been built on both good ground and poor, unsuitable ground. The results have been interesting.

In 2020, a beautiful house was constructed near the edge of a coastal area in the UK, but over time it couldn't sustain the damage caused by the weather, and it resulted in a disastrous collapse. It was valued at around £125,000, boasting an outdoor swimming pool. Today that house no longer exists, as it fell because of the unstable and unsafe land that it was erected on, and the homeowner has since found accommodation elsewhere.

Sand is a fascinating product used for gritting snowy roads, filling sandbags to prevent weather damage, and making glass, concrete blocks, bricks, and pipes. It can also used for water filtration. However, because the grains are too smooth and fine, it is one of the worst substances for building a suitable and strong house with, even though gritty sand is added to water and cement to make a paste in construction.

In a parable, Jesus spoke about two houses which were exposed to the same types of weather: rain, floods, and winds.

Any house that is built with suitable and durable materials should be able to withstand any kind of weather, provided it is built upon a strong, rocky foundation.

Jesus didn't mention the weather being fine and sunny, he only mentioned it being rainy and vehemently windy. That simply means that it is when the fierce winds and rains buffet the house that its integrity is tested, based on what it is built on and with. He further reminded us that when we hear his sayings and incorporate them into our own lives, we are like the man who builds on a sure foundation.

In fact, the reference to the house is intended to refer to individuals. We are the house. We live in our own personal bodies that are subject to physical deterioration as the years go by. We also live in bodies that are subject to psychological, emotional, physical, and spiritual attacks.

The cares of life can certainly take a toll on us in all sorts of various ways. There are things that come against us that knock is off our feet—things like sickness, alcoholism, death, financial devastation, relationship struggles, rebellious children, the inability to conceive, divorce, unemployment, economic hardship, sexual abuse, mental illness—the list is endless. Inside our 'houses', we are subjected to things that affect our souls mentally and spiritually, which can come in the form of attacks like character assassination or psychological and emotional pain.

With two different people exposed to the same 'elements', there are two different outcomes if one takes the Word of God seriously (on the rock) and the other hears and rejects his teachings and follows his or her own path (on sand).

The devil will tempt us children of God to throw in the towel, and he will throw a lot of things in our direction in order to get us to give up the race.

We need to know how we build our houses. We also need to be familiar with and knowledgeable about the type of spiritual materials to use to withstand the torrential storms of life. These storms can come in the form of metaphorical rain, wind, and floods—things that could potentially sink us or blow us away.

Even a ship is guided by the water beneath it, and yet it needs winds and stormy seas in order to reach its destination.

In prophecy, water represents people and wind symbolizes conflict. A lot of our trials here on earth generally revolve around our relationships with various sorts of people. Jesus wants us to live in love, harmony, and peace with them, if possible. The spiritual attacks will come, but if we take it to Jesus in prayer, he promises never to leave or forsake us. He promises to have our back and help us in our time of need. The psalmists David and Solomon said that 'the name of the Lord is a strong Tower, the righteous run into it and are safe' (Proverbs 18:10).

'Yea, and all that will live godly in Christ Jesus will suffer persecution' (2 Timothy 3:12). Many characters in the Bible left footprints of their lives as examples of people who built their lives on God's principles and commandments. Many of them are awaiting the First Resurrection, with the second death having no power over them. 'Blessed are they that do his commandments, that they may have right [permission] to the tree of life' (Revelation 22:14).

Jesus is the Rock and sure foundation. We are to build on him.

We are to embrace his teachings, his character, and his holy Word, which instructs us how to behave as saints of God whilst living here on earth. It's not enough to just hear or read his sayings; we must adhere to and believe his Word, living it into life.

We can be confident that when we cling to Jesus and build on him who loves us, we become anchored and unmoveable in him. It is true that we will be subject to the elements, which may cause us to cry or scream, or may even bring us down to our knees either in sorrow or worship. But because we are in Christ Jesus, we will survive, and he will repair any damage done.

Trials and troubles will and must come, but rest assured that because he has overcome tribulations, so shall we. We have an anchor that keeps the soul steadfast and sure while the billows roll. We are fastened to the Rock, which cannot move. We are grounded firm and deep in the Saviour's love.

We must build on the fruit of the Spirit, the beatitudes, stay in his Word, be filled with the Holy Spirit, and develop our relationship prayerfully with God on a daily basis.

There are many things that we know of Jesus that validate his claim to be a Rock. He is sure, firm, strong, true, faithful, unbiased, constant, unchangeable, and dependable, and he is all of these things to everybody for everyone who accepts him. He will not disappoint, deteriorate, or fail us. Because he has already been successfully tested and tried, we know that we can stand up against anything that comes our way, and he is our good example for us.

The house constructed on sand is the person whose life is built upon his or her own thinking, or the world's systems and philosophies. This person is plugged into a way that is devoid of God and his ways. The individual may be intellectual, affluent, and influential, or he or she may be normal and just getting by. Yet the cares of life keep the person grounded on a foundation that may outwardly look firm and stable but eventually, with time and stress, will not stand the test of time. The Lord's return will determine the eventual outcome.

Wet sand eventually hardens, dries out, and collapses. So it is with the system of the world. It may seem logical what the governmental systems endorse, but because their policies are not necessarily God-based, they will not endure. We are not to love the world or the things of the world, because doing so clashes with God's values.

There are people who have endured substantial and trying hardships, and have experienced severe traumas in their lives. These people know what it is to survive and cope against the odds. They try to be good spouses, parents, and workers. They know what it is to weep, put up a strong front, and grieve; they have known horrific abuse, depression, loss, sadness, rejection, and unhappiness. They've had to deal with addictions, fears, dysfunctional relationships, and manipulative behaviour. Some people reach for pills, alcohol, guns, or knives in order to self-mutilate or end it all. Some of these people go on to become saviours or advocates for other people who have gone through similar situations. God waits patiently for them to turn to him so they can receive total healing through his Son's blood.

God may test us and put us through spiritual obstacles to bring the best out in our lives. In various scriptures, we are encouraged 'to not despise the chastening of the Lord, because whom the Lord loves, he chastens.' In Hebrews 12:7–8, we are told, 'If you endure chastening, God deals with you as with sons; for what son is he whom the father chastens not? But if you are without chastisement, whereof all are partakers, then you are bastards, and not sons.'

The adversary doesn't care about what materials you choose to build on. It's more about whether you can stand, endure, or resist the 'weather' hurled at you, or whether you will buckle emotionally. 'Let every man take heed how he builds' (1 Corinthians 3:10).

For other foundation can no man lay than that is laid, which is Jesus Christ. Now if any man build upon this foundation gold, silver, precious stones, wood, hay, stubble; Every man's work shall be made manifest: for the day shall declare it, because it shall be declared by fire; and the fire shall try every man's work of what sort it is. (1 Corinthians 3:11–14)

Let us be careful how we build. Build upon the Rock, Jesus. He has an eternal reputation as the one who will not let you down no matter what life brings—whether good or ill. Sand does not endure.

Sandcastles and sculptures may look good, but after a while, when they dry out, they are easily destroyed owing to their composition and the weather. Cheap and inferior materials will eventually destroy your house.

On Christ the Solid Rock I stand; all other ground is sinking sand.

INNER COURTS AND PORCHES
(Based on 2 Chronicles 29)

KING HEZEKIAH WAS TWENTY-FIVE years old when he was crowned king. His father, Ahaz, who was king of Judah, began his reign at the youthful age of twenty. According to 2 Chronicles 28, Ahaz ruled for sixteen years (from 732 to 716 BC) in Jerusalem. But during that time, he walked in the same direction as the majority of the kings of Israel.

Ahaz introduced paganistic worship by making molten images to Baalim, burnt incense in the valley of Hinnom, and even burnt his children in the fire. He also sacrificed and burnt incense in the high places, on the hills, and under every green tree. He fared no better than the other Israelite kings, such as Ahab, Jehu, Jeroboam, Solomon, and Amaziah, who also engaged in idolatry during their reigns, worshipping nature and idols made of silver, gold, wood, and stone.

Because of his abominable acts, God punished him by delivering him into the hands of his Syrian enemies, who then took a great number of people captive as slaves in Damascus and brought them under extreme servitude. Why? Because they had forsaken the Lord God of their fathers. He affiliated himself to king Tiglath-Pileser of Assyria, for help, but he ended up being his subject instead.

Ahaz had a good example to follow in the eyes of Jotham, who had reigned before him. Jotham was a good king who ruled for sixteen years. But Ahaz had made a choice, even at such a young age, to do whatsoever was right in his own eyes. He did not regard the God of Abraham, Isaac, and Jacob but chose rather to worship graven images and work evil in the sight of God.

Ahaz was so evil that he even 'gathered together the vessels of the house of God, and cut in pieces the vessels of the house of God, and shut up the doors of the house of the Lord, and made himself altars in every corner of Jerusalem. And in every several city of Judah he made high places to burn incense unto other gods, and provoked God to anger' (2 Chronicles 28:24-25). So he was not only a worshipper but also an idolater. This man had no mind for God, to the extent that he destroyed and cut up the sacred objects used for worship that belonged in the Lord's house.

As a result, this man eventually died without God, and he was not given the honour of being buried amongst the most significant kings of Israel.

Fortunately, Hezekiah had a God-fearing mother named Abi-jah, whose name meant 'Whose father is Jehovah?'. She was a positively godly influence, which made all the difference to his leadership. She directed him skilfully into a righteous path and somehow managed to steer him away from her husband's unholy leanings.

When Hezekiah eventually ascended the throne in 716 BC, he had his work cut out for him in undoing all the sacrilegious mess that his father had left behind. One of the first initiatives that he decided to undertake was to combat the national stench of ungodliness that had permeated his kingdom. He was acutely aware of the spiritual decline in the land.

So in the first month of the first year of his reign, Abib opened the doors of the house of God and repaired them. He requested assistance from the priests and Levites to support the campaign. Hezekiah recognized what his father had done in Judea and how the inhabitants had enjoined themselves to the idolatrous practices without restraint.

Speaking to these men in the east street, he told them,

... our fathers have trespassed, and done that which was evil in the eyes of the Lord, and have forsaken him, and have turned away

61

their faces from the habitation of the Lord, and turned their backs. Also they have shut up the doors of the porch, and put out the lamps, and have not burned incense nor offered burnt offering in the holy place unto the God of Israel.' That's why the wrath of the Lord was upon Judah and Jerusalem' (2 Chronicles 29:6).

He further encouraged them and said, 'My sons, don't be negligent: for the Lord has chosen you to stand before him, to serve him, and that you should minister before him and burn incense' (2 Chronicles 29:11). Although the previous king, his father, had put the Lord's house to neglect by closing the doors of the temple and had deliberately destroyed the consecrated vessels, Hezekiah was now re-instating the men back into their ministerial duties and the restoration of the tabernacle system.

More than fifteen Levitical men gathered together with other like-minded men and sanctified themselves.

And the priests went into the inner part of the house of the Lord, to cleanse it, and brought out all the uncleanness that they found inside the temple of the Lord into the court of the house of the Lord. And the Levites took it, to carry it out outside into the brook Kidron. (2 Chronicles 29:16).

The priests set about to work by removing all the articles of uncleanness and pollution found within the temple. The Bible is not clear as to what exactly was removed. However, one may ascertain that the objects removed included anything that was an abomination to God. Some such items would be relics, handheld clay images of gods, artefacts, or materials that conflicted with the holiness of God. This would also have included anything that King Ahaz might have introduced into the temple during his reign.

Because the temple of the Lord was in such a filthy condition, those who served were absent and unavailable. In addition to this, God's immediate presence was missing. He is a holy God who has no association with unrighteousness or uncleanness, as much as the temple was his earthly habitation.

People were finding their own way of worship. They copied the king in serving idols and burning incense away from the temple, thus rendering the services of the Levitical priesthood futile. As a result, the doors were shut. The temple was in darkness, as the candlestick was no longer giving off its continual light. The incense was not being offered; neither were there any burnt offerings given in the holy place. This meant that no blood was being shed for the remission and forgiveness of sins committed.

We must be aware that the inner court did not include the holiest of holies, as this was an area restricted solely to the high priest. And this deep-cleaning procedure in that area alone didn't take a single day. The verses following tell us that they began in the first month on the first day and finished it eight days later. There was clearly a lot of rubbish that needed to be removed.

Things were physically carried away to the Kidron brook to be destroyed and eliminated. It was at this same brook that Moses sprinkled the dust of the golden calf into the river. The Israelites were forced to drink it as punishment for their unfaithfulness towards God. Whatever pollution existed before had to be removed in order for holiness to be restored in the temple.

The regime continued for a further eight days into the porch of the Lord. The porch was a short entrance into the temple. Many feet walked through it. Whatever images or pictures of uncleanness or ungodly paraphernalia were found there were also removed.

With the removal of uncleanness came the restoration of holiness. A lot of water was used to wash and cleanse the inner court and porch. The vessels that were used to administer before the Lord were also cleansed and sanctified for use within the ministry.

At the end of the sixteen days, the men told Hezekiah,

'We have cleansed all the house of the Lord, and the altar of burnt offering, with all the vessels thereof, and the shewbread table, with all the vessels thereof. Moreover all the vessels, which king Ahaz in his reign did cast away in his transgression, we have prepared and sanctified, and look, they are before the altar of the Lord' ... Hezekiah rose early and gathered the rulers of the city and went up to the house of the Lord' (2 Chronicles 29:18-20).

They brought seven bullocks, seven rams, seven lambs, and seven male goats for a sin offering for the kingdom, the sanctuary, and the nation of Judah.

A lot of blood was shed for the sins of the people. The priests received the blood and sprinkled the blood of the bullocks, rams, lambs, and goats around the altar. Reconciliation was made for all of Israel. Afterwards the Levites played cymbals, harps, and psalteries and gave God praise through music, praise, and thanksgiving for his mercy towards them.

When that was done, even more offerings were offered unto the Lord, like a chain reaction. In verse 32 we are told, 'And the number of the burnt offerings, which the congregation brought, was seventy thousand bullocks one hundred rams, and two hundred lambs.' This was in addition to the initial sacrifice! What had initially begun with the king ended up with the entire nation being involved in the process of righteous restoration. There were so many offerings delivered for the sacrifices that the Levites struggled to keep up with their duties. Copious amounts of blood were shed to redeem the entire congregation and nation.

What Can We Learn from These Verses?

After Jesus's abolition of the tabernacle system, he provided a full and free salvation; combined with a new and living way, by his death on the cross. This means that we have become the New Testament version of a living holy temple of the Lord God, where he can reside within us by way of the Holy Spirit. 1 Corinthians 6:17–18 says,

What? Don't you know that your body is the temple of the Holy Ghost which is in you, which you have of God, and you are not your own? For you are bought with a price: so then glorify God in your body, and in your spirit which are God's.

Everything must be in order. We must first sanctify our lives by committing our lives to Christ in daily devotion of prayer, praise, and applying his Word in our hearts. In Psalm 51, King David makes 'cleansing' requests to God with verses that state, 'Wash me, purge me with hyssop, create in me a clean heart, restore to me the joy of your salvation, deliver me from blood guiltiness. Be merciful to me, oh God ... blot out my transgressions.'

The blood of Jesus will clean us wholly, totally, spiritually from every sin and temptation. We must call and cry out for mercy, confess our faults and sins to the Lord, and repent with a turning away from sin. By these actions, the Lord will draw near to us as we draw nearer to him. Only then can we lift him up in prayer, petition, and praise from the heart, which is then acceptable unto the Lord.

What Could the Porch Represent in Spiritual Terms?

The porch could represent our hearts, minds, or mouths. After all, what defiles a man? According to Matthew 15:15–20,

Whatever goes into the belly and is cast out into the drought? But those things which come out of the mouth come forth from the heart; and they defile the man. For out of the heart proceeds evil thoughts, murders, adulteries, fornications, thefts, false witness, blasphemies: These are the things which defile a man: but to eat with unwashed hands doesn't defile a man.

The works of the flesh also make us spiritually unclean. Our inner man needs to be maintained with works of righteousness constantly, which whilst we are in this body is not easy. This is why we need the aid of the Comforter to keep us on track as we live in this world.

What Does This Mean for Us Today?

Everything in the tabernacle structure represented Jesus in one way or another. The lamps gave light and direction. The shewbread speaks of our communion and intimacy with God. The incense represents prayers and praise, which is worship to God. The sacrifice of the animal was the substitute for the individual who sinned, with the shedding of blood.

So, for the children of God, we too must offer the sacrifices of praise and thanksgiving. It will cost us something. Even when things don't happen the way they should, or when things go wrong, there must be a 'praise is what I do' attitude. It will reach to God as a fragrant smell, just as in the tabernacle system—before the smell of the blood even reached the veil of the holiest of holies.

We participate in fellowship with the Father when we have a right-standing relationship with him; walking and talking in union by living a righteous life that pleases him. God has also called us to be lights. Just as his Son is the Light of the World, so too we must shine the gospel in our lives and in our hearts, and guide people to Him.

God cannot, and will not, dwell in dirty vessels. Because the temple was contaminated with unholy objects, it was off limits to the Levitical administration; not even God could reside there. Although it was his dwelling place of sanctity, originally anointed with water, blood, and oil, it was replaced by a structure filled with abominable items and filth—He just couldn't remain there whilst those things were present.

As exhorted in the book of Leviticus 11:44 and 1 Peter 1:16, 'We must be holy, as he is holy.' We cannot expect God to receive our sacrifices, prayers, or praises from lives that are not totally consecrated and dedicated to him. In turn, he cannot bless us, as sin is an offence to him. That is why the shedding of blood was so important (and still is) with regard to making the sinner whole. By ultimately sending his son Jesus to fulfil this universal act, he has made it possible that all may have access to the wonderful gifts of his grace: forgiveness, mercy, reconciliation, peace, cleansing, anointing, and sanctification.

Historically, it took a period of time to remove all the filth and contamination found within the temple. Holiness certainly doesn't happen overnight. Change takes time. As we cooperate with the Holy Spirit, he enables us to make holiness possible, even in this serious and unpredictable era that we live in.

So first things first. We must engage in confession and repentance with cleansing by the Word, sanctification, and forgiveness through the blood of Jesus Christ. Then we must offer praise and thanksgiving to the Worthy One. Then we can progress unto dedicated righteous lives, ensuring that our inner man—the temple—is clean for the Lord's total residency through the Holy Spirit and that our mouths do not defile our outer man. What comes out of our mouths comes from our hearts, and it will either contaminate our lifestyle for holiness or glorify him. When we do this right, we become conduits of his greater glory and vessels of honour that he can use time and time again.

But in a great house there are not only vessels of gold and of silver, but also of wood and earth; and so to honour and some to dishonour. If a man purge himself from these, he shall be a vessel unto honour, sanctified, and suitable for the master's use, and prepared unto every good work. (2 Timothy 2:20:21)

May our inner lives and our hearts—the courts and inner porches—be accessible for the Master until he returns.

JACOB AND ESAU
(Based on Genesis 27)

G OD SAID TO ISAAC in a dream,
Stay in the land which I shall tell you of ... and I will make your seed to multiply as the stars of heaven, and I will give your offspring all these countries; and in your seed all the nations of the earth shall be blessed. Because that Abraham obeyed my voice and kept my charge; my commandments, my statues and my laws. (Genesis 26:4)

Isaac lived in Gerar, on the coast, south of Judah.

Genesis 25:22 states,

And the children struggled together within her, and she said, 'if it is so, why am I thus?' And she went to enquire of the Lord. And the Lord said to her, 'Two nations are in your womb, and two manner of people shall be separated from your bowels: and the one "people" shall be stronger than the other: and the elder shall serve the younger.'

Good move! Rebekah consulted and checked it out with God, who gave her a clear response. Jacob's name was fitting!

Was not Esau Jacob's brother? Says the Lord, yet I loved Jacob, and I hated Esau. (Malachi 1:3–4)

He ([Jacob] took his brother by the heel in the womb, and by his strength he had power with God.' [wrestling with the angel at the Jabbok brook, where he obtained a blessing and new name: Israel— Prince of God]. (Hosea 12:3)

There's something fascinating about Jacob. His name is

suggestive of someone who's an opportunist. Even when he was in his mother's womb, he was clutching what didn't belong to him. His early persistence paid off.

It is also interesting to note was that at birth he was not holding his brother's neck or hand, but his heel. This was not about friendship or murder, but he was grasping opportunity—authority from weakness. We've heard the expressions, 'at one's heel', meaning 'close behind,' and 'Achilles' heel', meaning a vulnerable weak point.

As the youngest son, Jacob came out into the world with an optimistic view of grasping good things. As Romans 9:11–12 puts it, '… it was said to her, (Rebekah), the elder (Esau) shall serve the younger (Jacob). Even though the children were not yet born, neither having done any good or evil, "that the purpose of God, according to election may stand not of works, but of him that calls."'

Genesis, from chapter 25 verse 27 onwards, charts their progress as fully grown men; very little was known about their relationship as children together. This verse reveals their specific characteristics. As twins, these men were very different both in characters and personalities: Esau was a cunning hunter, whilst Jacob was a 'plain' man who stayed indoors.

The stark differences between the two brothers was evident. When looking at this text, one may wonder what is wrong with hunting. Hunting is an outdoor pursuit, and something that can bring meat to the dinner table. There's also something about the thrill of the chase—the passion to chase, pursue, and finally capture what you have been running after.

Let us try to capture who Esau was as an individual. Had Esau tapped into spiritually hunting and pursuing God, his prospects would have been exceedingly great. Imagine him early every morning taking a snippet of food to his lips. He would then hurriedly exit the tent and go off into the outside world to see what he could capture. He was quite secure about his birthright as firstborn. He didn't have to earn it. But his heart was elsewhere—chasing.

Was his hunting wrong? Not necessarily. He was an excellent huntsman who procured venison for his father, who absolutely loved it when cooked. But his energy was always focused on what he could obtain outwardly for his flesh, but not for his spirit, whereas Jacob was an ordinary man. By cross-referencing the scriptures, I was led to the book of Job, chapter 1, verses 1 and 8, which outline a man who was upright, feared God, hated evil, and enjoyed staying indoors. Whether you are indoors or outdoors, you have time during which you can reflect and ponder upon life. Take time to build up a relationship with God. In the case of Jacob, it was a relationship with his parents, his immediate community, and God.

Jacob was an industrious and very hard-working man. This was evident in his service under his devious uncle Laban's employ. (See Genesis chapters 29–31). He worked consistently and conscientiously for him, working fourteen years for two daughters, plus six years for cattle (Genesis 31:38–41), He was studious and a great thinker—a man who respected his parents and had a heart for God.

Where Esau sought external pleasures, Jacob pursued internal, spiritual pleasures. And he was waiting for opportunity to knock. He was well aware that he was second to his twin brother, but he was likeminded in desiring the blessings that were denied him because of the automatic status his birthright gave him. Rebekah, who was very fond of Jacob, would doubtless have told Jacob of the day she gave birth to him and found him clinging to his brother's heel, and that God had revealed to her that two different people were in her womb.

Verse 29 of the chapter shows the domestic side of Jacob. He could cook! He boiled red pottage, a type of porridge or thick soup made of red lentils boiled in water. This is a savoury and highly nutritious dish which Arabs of the present day are especially fond of.

One day, Esau came home from the field and was very faint. Is it possible that on this particular day Esau caught nothing? If he did find game, did this hunt exhaust him more than usual? There seems to be no indication of a victory over a hunt on this occasion, but whatever the outcome, he was faint, suggesting that he was exhausted and tired.

Jacob had waited a long time for an opportunity like this and seized it in this vulnerable hour, when Esau's life was on the line and he badly wanted something to eat. Surely, had he caught something to eat, he needn't have bothered his brother for a morsel.

In a cry of desperation, Esau looked to his brother for salvation in the form of the red pottage. But Jacob, ever the strategist, spoke boldly and demanded, 'Sell me this day your birthright!' (Genesis 25:31). [Give me your privileges, benefits, your inheritance.] It was indeed a bold statement to make towards your brother in his hour of weakness. Hence, lay the snare.' Esau, the brilliant huntsman, who had an eye for attention and the knowledge to trap and capture, was now at the mercy of his quiet brother, who asked for something in return for sharing his meal. Notice that Jacob did not originally make the meal for Esau.

Unfortunately, it seemed that Esau had no bargaining chip to negotiate with. He had only his birthright. In a rash moment of haste, to satisfy the flesh and cure the hunger within, he trivially gave it away, without hesitancy or regard for his future. Furthermore, he sealed the agreement with a solemn verbal oath—an oath that was binding and couldn't be reversed.

After all, what did Jacob have to lose? He was stuck with a modest portion, whilst his careless brother had a double portion simply because he was born first. It provided special privileges and benefits to the heir. Esau's birthright was a very important and sacred thing. It belonged to the firstborn of the family. The family name and titles were to pass along to the eldest son. He would also receive a chief portion of the inheritance. But it was more than just a title to the physical assets of a family. It was also a spiritual position, and in the case of the people of God, God would lead the family, through the patriarchs' vision. (See Hebrews 1:1–2.)

In addition, in the special case of Esau and Jacob, this meant that the one to whom the birthright belonged was the one through whom the covenant promise made to their grandfather, Abraham, would be realized. Ultimately, the Messiah would come through the holder of the birthright and bless the nations of the earth. Esau was the firstborn, and the birthright was his, but like man, he failed to appreciate its value and sacredness.

71

Whilst Esau held the privileged position of having the double portion, Jacob was far from content. He took time out over the years of his growing up, reflecting on what could be his. And although his approach towards righteous gains was rather scheming and underhanded, he had a sincere motive. Matthew 6:33 encourages us to seek the kingdom of God, first and his righteousness, and all these things shall be added to you.

Seek those things which are above, set your affections, on things above. (Colossians 3:1)

He had the right idea.

For the most part, Esau spent most of his life chasing moving targets. He had a thirst for killing life. As a huntsman, his goal was to chase, kill, and make a meal for Dad. He was attracted to red—hence the red pottage—which was possibly a constant reminder of blood and the life that he continually took, violently, at any cost.

That he casually swore and handed his birthright over implied that he didn't really value the importance attached to it. However, he lived to regret it many years later. Interestingly enough, he was fitted out with the blessing of earth, and then heaven. His brother had heaven's dew and earth's blessing, in that order; which reflected where both their hearts were at.

Esau clearly did not learn his lesson. The second time around, the clever Jacob took away his blessing by agreeing with his mum to wear his brother's clothes. 'The voice is Jacob's voice, but the hands are then hands of Esau!'(Genesis 27:22).

Jacob wasn't content with his sole portion, and like Elisha, he pursued heavenly things and didn't give up. He seized a vulnerable opportunity to obtain something that wasn't his, and we don't see God telling him off about it either. Remember, God had already informed Rebekah that the 'elder would serve the younger' (Genesis 25:23).

From Jacob's life, I've discovered that it pays to serve Jesus and look up for heaven's rewards. It pays to chase God and pursue righteousness. This is unlike the life of Esau, who, as Hebrews chapter 12 puts it, was 'a profane person, who for just one morsel of meat sold his birthright. For we know how that afterward, when he would've inherited the blessing, he was rejected: for he found no place for repentance, though he sought for it carefully with tears.'

As children of the Most High God, when we accept Jesus as our Lord and Saviour, we automatically obtain privileges and birthright as fellow heirs of the kingdom of God.

> ... heirs of the kingdom of God. (Ephesians 1:3, 6)
> Power to become the sons of God. (John 1:12)
> Redemption through his (Jesus') blood. (Ephesians 1:7)
> The promise of eternal inheritance. (Hebrews 9:15)
> ... we inherit promises by faith. (Hebrews 6)
> I, the Lord, am your inheritance. (Numbers 18:20)
> In whom (Jesus) we have obtained an inheritance. (Ephesians 1:11)
> We are made partakers of Christ. (Hebrews 3:14)
> We are made partakers of the Holy Ghost. (Hebrews 6:4)
> Partakers of his holiness. (Hebrews 12:10)
> A partaker of the glory to be revealed. (1 Peter 5:1)

Sometimes we have people walking around being blessed who are ignorant of what God has placed within their lives, and instead of seeking God to show them and to have a relationship with him, they choose their own paths and destinies.

The 'Esaus' in life today run around chasing everything under the sun: girls; men; flashy cars; careers; gadgets; pleasures; treasures; holidays; hedonism; the drugs, sex, and rock 'n' roll culture; and trivial pursuits, and God doesn't figure in their chasing. Their chasing is meaningless. If you were to ask any celebrity whether he or she was happy, he or she would probably say yes (especially if he or she had a healthy bank account). But as celebrities grow older, they might seek a god to gain inner peace and contentment. Some may turn to Buddhism, Scientology, yoga, kabbala, New Age, mysticism, spiritualism, or psychics to enhance the peace that can come only from Jesus Christ. Unfortunately, in the day of trouble, their wealth will not save them. In fact, they will give it away and wish they had chosen the God path instead. 'What will it profit a man to gain the whole world and lose his own soul' (Luke 12:20).

Like Jacob, let us pursue our goodly and godly inheritance, which outlasts our lives here on earth, which are but temporary. The things of God are eternal and forever. Romans 6:23 tells us that 'the wages of sin is death, but the gift of God is eternal life through Jesus Christ our Lord.'

His grandfather, Abraham, had earlier warned his servant that his future in-laws should not come from the daughters of Canaan but from his own kindred. He didn't want his family to be polluted or intermingled with the paganistic values and practices of what God was arranging in his life.

Esau married two Canaanite wives and disregarded his parents' wishes for a pure, righteous bloodline. Tracing through his family tree, we discover that he fathered children who had a penchant for destroying lives, such as Amalek, Agag, and Herod the Great, to name but a few.

Esau didn't seem to care or value his righteous heritage; instead, he chose to mar it even though he was blessed. He negated his role and the rights of his birthright there and then. The fact that he disregarded it meant that after the selling of his birthright he didn't even look back and say, 'What have I done?' 'Did I really do that?' or 'I regret it.' He swore to it verbally, and his word was binding. There was no turning back until the event of the blessings that caused it to come back to mind.

Jacob	Versus	Esau
Long-term focus	Versus	Short-term focus
Futuristic	Versus	Temporal (here and now)
Spiritual	Versus	Carnal/Sensual
Second-born	Versus	Firstborn
Home-dweller	Versus	Hunter

Patience	Versus	Impatience
(Blessing) Given heaven first, then the earth after	Versus	(Blessing) Given the earth first, then heaven after.

Like Jacob, let us pursue our goodly and godly inheritance, which outlasts our lives here on earth, which are but temporary. The things of God are eternal and forever.

JOSEPH'S COAT OF MANY COLOURS

'NOW ISRAEL (JACOB) LOVED Joseph more than all his children, because he was the son of his old age; and he made him a coat of many colours' (Genesis 37:3). This is an interesting verse that carries a lot of profound truths in it. One of the questions one must ask is, Why was Joseph Jacob's favourite son? What had he done to deserve such favour? What made Jacob want to show off his younger son by placing him in a higher position within the family structure in the presence of his other older children?

Additionally, there were the possible repercussions for Jacob making a beautiful coloured coat and clothing Joseph in it. We discover much later on that he was making a loud statement with that garment. Although he was one of the youngest sons (Benjamin being the runt of the litter) and Reuben was his eldest child—which generally specified automatic birthright and greater inheritance—it would seem that Jacob had other plans. Was it possible that God had given him some kind of clue as to who the next deliverer would be?

There is a relational price to be paid when sibling rivalry enters families, especially when it is due to parental favouritism. The scriptures immediately start with the brothers Cain and Abel, of whom the latter was slain by the former. Then you have Jacob and Esau—two very different characters with two very different outcomes. There was David with his many children by his different wives. This was a very difficult household to manage, because the heir apparent didn't survive long after his distorted liaison with his half-sister Tamar. Adonijah seemed a promising prospect, but God had already found a king in the form of Solomon, who would then go on to build the promised house for the Lord. Absalom, who was David's darling son, revolted against his father and was eventually killed by Joab whilst his hair got tangled up in a big oak tree.

In a situation where preferential love and treatment are manifested towards an individual child, this would cause obvious tension, jealousy, resentment, and hatred amongst the siblings. On top of that, Joseph was also the offspring of Jacob's union with his favourite wife, Rachel. Consequently, his other ten step-brothers would have no real connection to him, save Benjamin, his other biological brother through Rachel.

Jacob showed his special love for his son Joseph by giving him a coat—not an ordinary coat, but one that reflected many colours. It was beautiful! He was clothed in a symbol of what was yet to come in the future. Why a coat? This coat depicted a mantle of authority and leadership. It was also an external representation of Joseph's overall life, though he was yet still a young lad. He was probably about sixteen or seventeen years old when he received it. The colours represented the multifaceted layers of his character and personality.

God did the same thing by giving Jesus the Holy Spirit at his baptism, which visibly descended on him in the form of a dove. He was vested with the power and authority to do many things.

The Spirit of the Lord God is upon me, because the Lord has anointed me to preach good tidings unto the meek; he has sent me to bind up the broken-hearted, to proclaim liberty to the captives, and the opening of the prison to them that are bound; To proclaim the acceptable year of the Lord ... (Isaiah 61:1–2 and Luke 4:18)

Throughout the world, colours communicate to us every day in different ways. For example, red can represent danger, a command to stop, passion, fire, blood, meat, and heat. Yellow can represent vibrancy, happiness, or a command to pause. Blue can represent serenity, peace, harmony, coldness, royalty, or something of a clinical nature. White can represent purity, cleanliness or hygiene, and righteousness.

As we explore the scriptures from Genesis chapters 37 through to 50, we discover a whole host of character traits found in this man Joseph. Much of these came about through his employment by others (to perform menial tasks and duties) and whilst he submitted himself to all kinds of social encounters.

In chapter 37, he appears as a spoilt brat. He may have been quite naive in flaunting his new garment in front of his older siblings. What a mistake that was.

One of the colours of Joseph's life was the gift of dreams and the ability to interpret their meanings. He shared a couple of them with his family, and they seemed to portray him as some kind of leader. The brothers naturally understood this and hated him even more for it.

He was an obedient child—well behaved, but a bit of an informer. He would inform his dad of his brothers' misdemeanours. As a spy, he was dangerous and couldn't be trusted. Dad always seemed to know what the big kids were up to!

But by the end of the chapter (37), Joseph's beautiful coat; which reflected the diverse abilities and attributes of Joseph's life, has been stripped off his body and smeared in a goat's blood. The brothers hated not only their brother but the coat too. They had to make their father believe that his favourite son was now dead.

(Jesus similarly had his purple robe stripped from his body. The soldiers drew lots and divided his garment whilst he hung on the cross [Matthew 27:28, 31, 35].)

Joseph was covered by the blood of Jesus. His life was not over, and his brothers overplayed their hands on his life. It didn't matter what they did to the coat; Joseph's inward life would be refined through the tests and struggles that confronted him.

The Colour and Characteristics of Joseph's Life

There is nothing stating that when Joseph was thrust into the hands of the Ishmaelite merchants for twenty pieces of silver he didn't resist them or struggling to escape or fight for his life. It was a quiet submission of his fate. Judah made that choice also.

(Here too is Jesus's life reflected. He was sold for thirty pieces of silver at the hand of his 'friend' Judas. He did not resist arrest but surrendered humbly to his fate. [See Colossians 3:12; 1 Peter 5:5].)

During his employment to his master, Potiphar, the captain of the guard and an officer of Pharaoh, Joseph was industrious, meticulous, and a dutiful servant in a foreign land. He accepted his role and put his new-found administrative skills to use. At over seventeen years of age, he proved himself to be competent, pragmatic, conscientious, diligent, responsible, proactive, reliable, and trustworthy. Other 'colours' of his life shone through: faithfulness, motivation, efficiency, a hard-working nature, thoroughness, and obedience.

God added grace and favour so that even his employer recognized that there was something extraordinary about him, and whatever he did flourished. Subsequently, he was promoted to the role of overseer within Potiphar's household. God was likewise pleased with Joseph's behaviour. It didn't matter that he was a servant; he was making the best use of his time by focusing his efforts on how to be a good steward to his boss. God blessed Joseph's achievements. Even with additional responsibility, he didn't let it go to his head, but he worked remarkably well, and everything that Potiphar had in the home and field was unusually prosperous and successful. (see Genesis 39:2-6)

Not long afterwards, Potiphar began to take a keen new interest in this handsome and unusual Hebrew man. He was undoubtedly attractive with good structure and an athletic physique. With her womanly wiles, she tried to seduce him. She used every trick in her book, including her speech, her touch, and deliberate attempts to be alone with him. (See Genesis chapter 39, verses 11–13). When Joseph refused her advances, she sulked and told her husband, accusing Joseph of sexual harassment.

79

Here another colour shines through: integrity. 'Don't commit adultery.' Although the Ten Commandments did not come into existence until the children were at the foot of Mount Sinai, man still knew the consequences of sin. 'Flee fornication.' 'Flee youthful lusts.' 'Cleave to that which is good.' Joseph did well in the presence of sexual temptation. We don't know how long the flirtatious wife went on with this charade, but God made a way that day when she was left holding his garment in her hand. Potiphar, after investigation, placed Joseph in prison for his alleged crime.

In Genesis 39:18-23 we read something insightful. Although Joseph was wrongfully accused, he didn't throw a tantrum, demand a lawyer, or seek compensation. Rather, he accepted this trial of faith and allowed God to help him through. He was resilient under pressure and injustice.

God honoured him in jail by giving him a role within the prison so that even the warden was happy for him to take over with full authority. The whole place was in his hands to do with as he saw fit. He was faithful in a posh house; he was faithful in a jailor's role. The prison was another foundational course of people management.

As an administrator for the prison, he would have perfected his project management skills as a welfare officer and accounts manager, and he would have become adept at budgeting, catering, bedding, staffing, and maintenance, improving the prisoners' lives. Matthew 20:26 says, '... whoever will be great among you, let him be your minister (servant). And whosoever will be chief among you, let him be your servant.' This training took around a decade. This was a rehearsal for an upcoming event.

Joseph's life was a series of dips and peaks. He left home, was placed in the pit (down), was employed with Potiphar (up), was put in jail (down), and became governor of Egypt (up).

In Genesis chapter 40, Joseph uses his gift of revealing dreams with two men, achieving two different outcomes. He is forgotten by the one released on Pharaoh's birthday. But his time to shine comes again in chapter 41. With God's help, Joseph gave the meaning of the Pharaoh's dreams and suggested that he find someone faithful with administrative skills and operational management expertise to preside over the distribution of foods during the seven-year famine.

When Joseph had explained the dream, he even offered practical suggestions and advice as to what Pharaoh needed to do to save the lives of his people during the famine ahead. Here we observe the diplomacy, humility, wisdom, knowledge, and understanding that were bestowed upon Joseph because he trusted in God and had a true relationship with him.

In response to the explanation of the dream, Pharaoh did the right thing by suggesting that this same person, Joseph, be the officer. This was what God had in mind all along. His training in prison was the basis of the experience he needed in order to meet the needs of the people outside his community. Once, he had been hidden from view, practising and learning how to manage people, but now he was on a full-scale platform, meeting the needs of the Egyptians, his family, and the neighbouring countries also affected by the famine.

In one day, the following transformation took place.

- Joseph, a humble man, was exalted (showing humility before honour).
- He was chief but also a servant.
- He was given the role of prime minister—a position second only to that of Pharaoh.
- Pharaoh gave Joseph his own ring, signifying power and authority (Genesis 41:42).
- Pharaoh gave Joseph new garments of linen befitting his office.
- Pharaoh placed a gold chain around Joseph's neck (showing prominence and honour).
- Pharaoh gave him a chariot to ride in, providing transport and signifying honour.
- Pharaoh gave Joseph a new name, 'Zaphnath-Paaneah', meaning 'the man to whom secrets are revealed'.
- Joseph was given a wife called Asenath, who was the daughter of Potipherah, a priest of On.

At the age of thirty, Joseph was well-developed, refined, experienced, discreet, honourable, wise, and accountable, and he finished his schooling and discipline with flying colours—no certificate required.

Although the coat that was given back to his father was marred with blood as sign of his death, it was finally exchanged with another coat of prestige, power, and authority that reflected all the nuances of Joseph's character traits. In fact, there are about sixty references and similarities that link his life to Jesus, based on his life alone!

Another colour Joseph acquired is mercy, along with evidence of kindness, forgiveness, and goodness. After thirteen years away from his brothers, his features would've changed significantly. He would appear more masculine and mature in appearance than the young lad they had sold into foreign hands. There is no doubt that he was fluent in the Egyptian language and very good at what he executed.

When famine finally struck Egypt, as foretold, Canaan was also crippled with severe food shortages. The brothers were forced to visit Egypt, where they heard there was a good source of ample food. Through this medium, Joseph was able to extract information concerning his father's welfare, his brother Benjamin, and their current behaviour. He was also able to discern whether his brothers had changed or repented of their deeds.

He showed mercy in giving them corn without charging them for it. (Genesis 4:1-3)

He hid his identity well and used an interpreter to reach them. But he left sufficient subtle clues of his identification without revealing them (Genesis 42:16–20). He made generous provisions for the entire family in the land of Goshen, where they lived. Neither did he retaliate when the opportunity presented itself (Genesis 42:24).

He showed hospitality and kindness with a feast. And because shepherds were an abomination to Egyptians, he sat away from them (Genesis 42:30–32).

He arranged the seating so that the brothers sat according to their birthdates. He demonstrated true forgiveness and reconciliation in (Genesis 43:32-33).

He recognized that he was fulfilling his God-given purpose. By engaging in self-denial, he allowed his interpersonal skills and gifts to be channelled for the greater good towards the needs and welfare of the people he served, to maximum effect.

The colours of Joseph's life came into maturity as he lived among people and catered for their needs. He had a genuine interest in their welfare and was made perfect through his sufferings. He was positive, and his actions affected everyone beneficially.

His message of love spoke volumes: 'You thought evil against me, but God meant it for good' (Genesis 50:20).

God gives us significance, power (through the Holy Spirit), and authority to be sons and daughters of him. He clothes us in attitudes of righteousness through sanctification. He gives us new names and blesses us alongside our trials, beyond our wildest dreams.

We have colours in our own lives that are shaped by our childhood, upbringing, and environmental circumstances. It's what we choose to do with our personalities that develops us to be whatever God wants us to be.

What is your pressing desire? What burns within you? What has God called you to do? What are you character colours of your life?

Joseph's Coat

The coat given to Joseph by his father Jacob was truly beautiful, yet we see the characters of his life reflected by the many interpersonal skills, giftings and other qualities, which made his personality colourful within and without as listed below. Perhaps, you can add to the list.

- diligence
- wisdom, knowledge, and understanding
- mercy
- integrity
- administration

- revelation of dreams
- duty, hospitality
- loyalty, kindness
- perseverance
- self-control
- patience
- goodness
- industriousness
- competence
- pragmatism
- meticulousness
- responsibility
- reliability
- efficiency
- trustworthiness
- diplomacy
- confidentiality
- manageriality
- humility
- intelligence
- submissiveness (in employment)
- discernment
- generosity
- forgiveness
- obedience
- resourcefulness
- honesty
- sensitivity
- compassion
- optimism
- focus

My, what a beautiful coat!

HOW TO BE AN EFFECTIVE MANAGER

(Based on the Life of Joseph in Egypt, Genesis 39)

T HE QUESTION IS, 'CAN I be trusted with something or someone that is within my grasp or reach but is off limits?' There are different angles of looking at this question. For instance, a person who has a financial career in a position of trust earns a good wage and yet feels comfortable enough to steal thousands of pounds right from under their employer's very nose.

We must always remember that what Joseph went through in chapter 39 was essentially, and most importantly, a test. It was crucial for Joseph to pass it because it determined both whether he could be trusted not to touch another person's property (as in Potiphar's wife) and whether he was ready for higher levels of responsibility.

Joseph was very discerning, and he recognized not just the huge fleshly potential but also the damaging consequences of his actions. By this test, he proved to God and himself that he was able to control his impulses regarding adultery and fornication.

We must consider that when spouses are away at work, it is tempting and possible to strike up an affair with someone, whether for the sheer thrill of it or even to cause mischief. But unfortunately, it always leads to disappointment, divorce, murder, jealousy, anger, and even breakups within interrelationships.

Because he passed the sexual temptation test, God deliberately promoted Joseph in the prison system so that he could learn some more lessons which would further prepare him for the much bigger picture that he had in store for him. God will usually place you in an environment that will develop and stretch your abilities (as long as you allow him to).

Sadly, sexual integrity is an area where a lot of men and women fall down. We do so well and then someone comes along who finds us interesting and wants something more than a friendship. (This is depicted in the 2003 film *Bruce Almighty*, featuring Jim Carrey, when Bruce eventually clinches the position of anchor-man and becomes successful, causing the female presenter he liked to fancy him all of a sudden, though initially she was not interested in him at all.)

Potiphar held a new fascination for this handsome Hebrew employee who seemingly worked industriously and conscientiously for his master, and now he made a great impression on her. She wanted so him badly that she moved seductively around him and made it known that she wanted a sexual relationship. This illicit affair would have negatively sealed the fate of the Israelites, had Joseph participated. Pharaoh had entrusted Joseph to manage his household affairs, not his wife!

And it came to pass after these things, that his master's wife cast her eyes upon Joseph; and she said, 'Lie with me'. (She was so brazen, and bold about making her intentions clear about what she wanted from him). But he refused, and said unto her, Behold, my master doesn't know what is with me in the house, and he has committed all that he has into my hand. There is none greater in this house than I; neither has he kept back any thing from but you, because you are his wife: how then can I do this great wickedness, and sin against God? (Genesis 39:7–9)

She challenged him to make love to her, whilst he challenged her and informed her that that act was great wickedness. She went to great pains to flirt with him, creating opportunities where she could be alone with him and using the language and behaviour of harlotry, hoping that he would eventually cave into temptation.

Joseph's integrity was at stake. The lust of the flesh has its temporary rewards of sexual satisfaction hidden away from the eyes of men but is viewed as unlawful, harmful, and sinful in the eyes of a holy God. Thankfully, Joseph honoured God with his ability to focus on the consequences of sinful and wilful behaviour. Considering that he was working in an environment where he was daily exposed to someone who desired him, who wanted an affair, and who was by all means sexually harassing him, he demonstrated tremendous integrity and tenacity on his part.

He clearly understood that engaging in such an adulterous affair would not only take him out of the will of God but would also expose him to the vices of deception, dishonesty, sin, lies, a possible pregnancy, hypocrisy, accusations of rape, and possibly murder.

Arguably, at this stage it would've been understandable for Joseph to and complain, or even to have a pity party about being wrongfully charged and sent to prison. After all, he was innocent of the charges made against him.

Nonetheless, his attitude and approach towards the injustice done were admirable. Here he was, in a foreign land, away from his home and family. He had worked as a slave employed under Potiphar, had been accused of sexual harassment, and then had been thrown into jail to await his fate. Yes, he had every reason to complain and sue for the injustice given, if he wanted to. Yet he somehow came to understand later on that God had made a way of escape for him through this divine route. He had delivered him out of a very dangerous liaison and had placed him into a more suitable environment for his next training and developmental programme.

Servants, be subject to your masters with all fear and respect. Not only to the good and gentle, but also to the forward. For this is the thankworthy, if a for conscience toward God and endure grief, suffering wrongfully. For what praise is it, if when you are buffeted for your faults, you shall take it patiently? But if you do well, and suffer for it, you take it patiently, this is acceptable with God. (1 Peter 2:20)

For even unto this you have been called: because Christ also suffered for us, leaving us an example, that you should follow his steps:

who did no sin, neither was guile found in his mouth. Who, when he was reviled, reviled not again; when he suffered he threatened not; but committed himself to him (God) who judges righteously' (1 Peter 2:23).

In Genesis 39:20, Potiphar placed Joseph in a prison facility where the king's prisoners were retained (the professional, elite, highly trained servants). But in verse 21, we see a glimmer of hope: 'Whereby, the Lord was with Joseph, and showed him mercy (in the form of visible kindness and goodness) and gave him favour in the sight of the keeper of the prison (prison warden/officer).' (Genesis 39:21).

This verse follows: 'And the prison officer committed to Joseph's hand all the prisoners that were in prison; and whatsoever they did there, he was doer of it!' (Genesis 39:22)

When God shows you favour, *it is like getting the red-carpet treatment.* He will allow strangers to empower you and give the respect that you've shown to others. You'll be given special privileges without even asking for them.

Verse 23 states, 'The prison officer looked not to anything that was under his hand; (he saw that) the Lord was with Joseph, and that which he did, the Lord made it to prosper.' (See Psalm 1:3 ['he shall be like a tree ... fruits in his season ... whatsoever he does shall prosper'].)

'And whosoever will be chief among you, let him be your servant' (Matthew 20:27). This was just where God wanted Joseph to be. It was the next phase of his training and development course and assignment. Because the sex test was important in terms of integrity, honesty, accountability and trust, God was saying, 'You are now ready to start rehearsing for the role and assignment that I have in store for you. I want you to undergo another season of intense training and honing of all your interpersonal skills, with regard to looking after the welfare of my people. They have various concerns and issues. I want you to discover what they need and make them comfortable, acceptable, and in touch with themselves and society again. Love them and teach them. Find ways of improving the conditions they are in, and watch the results. Don't worry about making mistakes either, because as you make your trials and errors, you will be making good decisions and finding out what solutions work best.

'Because you honoured my word when you were tempted, I will exalt you. I will always be there for you. If you have any problems, talk to me about them, and I will share strategies with you so they will work out effectively and successfully. Because I am with you, no man will stand against you. If anything, men will approve all your wishes, plans, ideas, and suggestions, because there're already approved by me.

'So go ahead, Joseph; don't sit and stew. I'm teaching you the ministry of servanthood. I will reward you greatly in the end, so don't worry about payments or accolades for now. When this is over, your name and fame will be great. In the meantime, just enjoy this role away from the public glare until I give you the green light. I have empowered you to do so. I love you, Joseph, and my word is ready and steady.'

God wanted Joseph to learn the lessons of

- putting the needs and concerns of others before himself;
- practising self-denial and giving sacrificial time to those who well deserved it (as there were people there who had committed crimes);
- developing patience, tolerance, and temperance—in fact, the whole fruit of the Spirit—and
- perfecting his administrative aspects and people skills—interpersonal relationships.

One of the first key tasks Joseph faced was to understand and pinpoint the concerns of the prisoners. He would do this by taking a genuine interest in their complaints, by listening carefully, and by constructing ideal and strategically tailored solutions wherever possible.

He would have logged information and carefully detailed areas for improvement within the prison confines. Over time, he would have learned to speak the Egyptian language fluently in order to reason and converse better with his peers and become well-versed in the culture of their everyday lives.

He would have developed various forms of infrastructure, setting out new and flexible policies, standards, and norms, in order to positively deliver better services to the prisoners' daily lives. Imagine Joseph hard at work employing various ideas and techniques, initiating new reforms, and managing his chores with the flair of an official prison officer! He may have possibly covered aspects like these, for instance:

Health records	Physical exercise	Social care
Personal hygiene	Counselling	Finances and budgeting
Infection control	Education and training	Complaints and grievances
Work and career opportunities	Rehabilitation	Various reforms
Visitation rights	Disciplinary laws	Security and protection
Incentives for prisoners	Conflict resolution	Food and catering

It is rarely heard of for a prison officer to just hand over the keys and allow someone else to run the system by totally revamping it, incorporating different methods, and introducing new guidelines of how to look after criminals. But you see, this was the finger of God, and his purpose was revealed much later on. Joseph was probably in his early twenties when he began this new assignment, full of ideas and energy in applying societal and practical standards within the very walls of the prison he served in. He was in charge, and he was busy administering to the welfare of people who were likely much older than him!

Joseph understood that the position he was in was a highly esteemed one which commanded respect. He also knew it was right for him to earn it. For instance, being arrogant towards the inmates would not have been beneficial in the push for things to become successful. Pride and anger, aggression, and violence were deemed useless for the running of a smooth organization.

Most importantly, the work was hidden from view. It was here where he could make errors and mistakes that could be corrected away from the glaring public's eyes. When he had finished training, he was prepared and equipped to face the world with a head full of strategies. This reminds me of Acts 1:8b: '... and you shall be witnesses of me both in Jerusalem and all Judea, and in Samaria, and unto the uttermost part of the earth.'

Joseph's ministry was hidden and revealed. This divine project was going to extend towards the outskirts of Egypt. This pagan nation was soon to become a saviour to other nations based on one man—Joseph. Primarily, it began in his first employment with Potiphar, as a taster; it then carried on for almost eleven years while he was honing his skills in prison. And finally it continued on the grand stage outside the confines of the prison in Egypt.

As time went by, Joseph waited on two men in particular: a butler and a baker who were employees of Pharaoh. One can immediately tell that Joseph was a people person by his concern for them. They shared their dreams, which Joseph predicted with amazing accuracy from God. He asked the butler to put in a good word to Pharaoh so Joseph could be released from prison. But unfortunately, the butler forgot. Joseph's time for release was not ready.

Then something amazing happened. Pharaoh had a dream so bizarre that not even his magicians or soothsayers could make heads or tails of it. Because the dream was from God, there was only one man to offer the meaning—Joseph.

When your training programme is completed and you have covered all the necessary requirements for the assignment, *God will personally call for you.* Think about the lives of Esther and David. One moment they were living ordinary lives, hidden out of view, and then they were suddenly catapulted into the spotlight.

When Pharaoh had exhausted himself of all his experts, the butler recalled his incident in prison. Joseph was called, and he explained the interpretation of the dream, predicting a famine would hit Egypt severely. He offered good counsel, along with some sound practical suggestions and solutions. Pharaoh recognized that this man was suitable for the task and endowed him with honour, power, and authority as governor of Egypt.

Joseph's administrative skills had been naturally honed through his experiences inside the prison walls. As a result, owing to a careful planning strategy, the lives of many were preserved throughout the seven years of famine. All were fed and those around and outside the country were able to find food in the land of Egypt. Joseph looked after the world around him.

When Jacob got wind that there was food in Egypt (as they, too, experienced food shortages in the land of Canaan), he urged his ten sons to travel there so they could benefit from the land's supply. The brothers did so, paying homage to Joseph as the prime minister, just as his dreams had suggested. Eventually the entire family moved up into Egypt and were given the fertile land of Goshen.

In Jesus's prophecy in Isaiah 61:1–2, he outlines his ministry one day during service in the synagogue. 'The Spirit of the Lord God is upon me, because the Lord has anointed me to preach good tidings to the meek; he has sent me to bind up the broken-hearted, to proclaim liberty to the captives, and the opening of the prison to them that are bound.'

Jesus likewise fulfilled his mandate, right down to giving up his life as a sacrificial lamb for the sins of the world. Interestingly, there is no passage in scripture that literally tells of an event where Jesus took prisoners out of prison, so this portion must have a different meaning. People were imprisoned by their conditions: leprosy, sin, blindness, palsy, demonic possession, wrong thinking, lameness, and death. Jesus liberated them all and gave them new reason to live again. He challenged wrong behaviour and concepts by using parables to bring out spiritual truths. Often people left confused, not really understanding what he meant, whilst others took him for a prophet as he spoke with conviction and great authority.

Jesus's mission was to train twelve ordinary men over a period of three and a half years to continue the work he had begun, before returning to heaven. He developed a framework in which his disciples were empowered to do what he did. He gave them instructions on how to behave, what to do, and what to expect. (See Matthew 10:1–28). It was a ministry of care. They were to be as wise as serpents and as harmless as doves, with characteristics of sheep.

Today, God is calling his people to action. We are initially to be concerned about the welfare of our immediate fellow brethren. As we practise this, it becomes easier when showing mercy to those outside who are our potential brothers and sisters.

Each of us has been endowed with special heavenly spiritual gifts to be handled with care and incorporated within and outside of the body of Christ. There are ministries of help, including counselling, education, and voluntary services. Some other ways to help include the following:

- Befriend someone and offer assistance where possible.
- Organize crèches, or nurseries for toddlers.
- Provide help within the homes of the sick, elderly, or depressed.
- Donate financial support to charities.
- Become a mentor or life coach.
- Cater to the needs of the homeless, hungry, and neglected.
- Teach parenting skills to new single mothers or parents.
- Lead Bible studies.
- Engage in prison ministry.

Some Points to Consider

When an opportunity presents itself for you to go against your better instincts, will you steal? Will you manipulate or control a situation to your advantage? Will you lie to cover up your 'crimes'? Will you violate trust placed in your care? Do you consider the consequences of your actions based on your intentions? Can you stand your ground when the odds are against you? Are you prepared to forgive your debtors and move on? Do you recognize the opportunities within the situations you face and the huge potential for growth?

Make allowances for failure; it's all part of the assignment. In tricky moments, consult God. Will you violate someone's rights in order to satisfy your own? Be prepared to serve in areas where you feel unlikely to fit in. Do you love and respect people? This is a strong indication of how you view yourself and God.

When left to yourself, will you violate a confidence or trust placed in you to satisfy your own urges, disregarding any subsequent punishment? When you violate trust, you end up hurting yourself in the process even though the damage is done to another individual. Any breach of trust is a violation of rights towards another individual and yourself.

Any employer seeks an individual who is honest, is of good character, is faithful, and won't abuse his or her rights overtly or covertly.

Be hospitable. If doing so gives you grief, turn the other cheek. Don't retaliate (although this is much easier said than done).

Let us remember that you were once imprisoned in trespasses and sin, and the same invitation of forgiveness, mercy, and salvation is available to all who will receive it.

First Corinthians 13 is the love chapter, which informs the reader of what love is and what love is not. We are encouraged to practise it daily, because it is upon these principles that the church is being attacked. And it will continue to be attacked if we fail to keep up communion with the Father and with each other.

Finally, we are called to be faithful stewards, acknowledging that God is Lord of everything and everyone, including powers and Satan. And like Joseph, he expects us to be committed, loyal, honest, obedient, humble, and diligent in whatever he chooses for us to undertake. He promises to sustain us, especially during the difficult times in our lives.

THE TRANSITION OF PRINCESS MICHAL FROM LOVE TO HATE

THE BACKDROP TO THIS story is relevant in highlighting the overall development of the relationship between David and Michal.

We are first introduced to Princess Michal in 1 Samuel 18:20. She was one of two sisters, the other one being Merab. She was the daughter of King Saul, son of Kish, of the tribe of Benjamin, who was anointed king by the prophet Samuel. We don't know a great deal about her, but we can glean some insights into her life.

Verse 20 says, 'And Michal loved David: and they told Saul, and the thing pleased him.'

By this time, David was installed in the palace as the court musician and armour bearer to King Saul. He was in unfamiliar surroundings, away from the sheepfold. Not long afterwards, he become the national champion in town who had bravely killed a giant by decapitating him with just a stone and a catapult. His heroism had not gone unnoticed by Michal.

Saul initially had intentions of marrying him off to his older daughter, Merab, as was customary then, but it didn't work out like that in the end. She was eventually married off to a man called Adriel the Meholathite.

The scriptures make it clear that Michal loved David. This was more than just gazing at his handsome features; she was attracted to his personhood. This anointed, lovely, and sensitive young man had some outstanding qualities.

When Saul put the proposal of marriage to him, David admitted that he was happy to be his son-in-law, but he was unable to provide a dowry for the attractive Michal, because he was a poor man. He was the youngest member of his family, barely made any money, and had not long ended his occupation as a shepherd.

But Saul had other sinister plans that he was conjuring up in his mind. He had heard the songs in the street: 'Saul had slain his thousands, and David his ten thousands' (1 Samuel 18:7), and that really grated him right into his soul.

In response to finding a way for David to gain his bride, he suggested that David go and kill the Philistines for him—just one hundred of them—and, as a dowry, to bring back their foreskins as proof of their deaths. There was an ulterior motive hidden here. Saul had hoped that David would die in battle. He had tackled one very large man on a grand scale—Goliath. Now Saul was asking him to go into battle full-on and slay Israel's enemies. He came back alive and collected not just one hundred foreskins, but a staggering two hundred. And yes, the tokens were counted, and so David was given permission to marry Michal.

At that point, Saul's paranoia had grown another string—fear. He was afraid of David, who seemed to be undefeatable. He was running out of options, so another strategy he tried was to promote him as leader of the army. The only problem for Saul was that David kept coming back alive. Another verse points out that Michal, Saul's daughter, loved him.

Even after the wedding shortly afterwards, there was still a wind of tension blowing from Saul towards David.

David hadn't put a foot wrong. Everywhere he turned, he behaved wisely, whether on the battlefield, among fellow soldiers much older than himself, in the community, or even in the palace. He gained the respect of the people all around him, and he was celebrated as an accomplished young man with a lot of things going for him.

Despite all of this, Saul was desperately trying to kill him and had even dragged his servants into his paranoid behaviour. One day, whilst Saul was in one of his foul moods, he tried to pin David to the wall with his javelin, but David escaped. Things intensified as Saul sent messengers to David's house to watch him and slay him. Michal, with loving concern told him, '[Darling,] If you don't save your life tonight, tomorrow you will be slain.' (1 Samuel 19:11). She let him out of the window, and in order to protect her new husband further, she covered up for him by placing a decoy covered with goats' hair in his bed. That episode caused even further friction between Michal and her father.

Another family member named Jonathan, the eldest son of Saul, had also developed a special bond with David. Jonathan loved David too, just as he loved his own soul. This kind of love was a strong 'philia' love between friends.

In this rather complex triangle, we discover that Michal adored her husband, and so did Jonathan, to the extent that he made a pact with him to show kindness to his family. And right in the middle is Saul, who initially loved David but now had transformed into being his constant enemy. Why? Because he secretly knew that one day the kingdom would be his.

David's life was in danger. He was a fugitive in Canaan running away from Saul, who was sometimes at his heels. Saul chased him over hill and vale with his chosen men. Saul was no longer receiving any prophetic assistance or dreams, even though he had the gift of prophecy himself. The Spirit of God had replaced his gift with an evil spirit that bothered him. It was a sad state of affairs.

Now that God had officially anointed David as king, he left Saul to his own devices. While Saul should have been reigning from a kingly position, he spent most of his years chasing the 'king in the wings'. It was an intense season of refinement, which helped to equip David for kingship in the future.

It was very difficult at times, but David always put his faith in God. When you read the journals of his walk with God, you realize just how sensitive, raw, and real he was in his relationship with him. Today we are encouraged by many of the psalms he penned, sometimes under extreme circumstances. For example:

'I will bless the Lord, at all times, his praise shall continually be in my mouth.' (Psalm 34:1)

'The Lord is my Shepherd, I shall not want.' (Psalm 23:1)

'Oh, Lord my God, in thee do I put my Trust: save me from all them that persecute me, and deliver me' (Psalm 7:1).

'I cried unto the Lord, with my voice, and he heard me out of his holy hill' (Psalm 3:4).

'I will love you, Oh Lord, my strength!' (Psalm 18:1)

Furthermore, when you read through the story of David's life leading up to Saul's eventual death, you find that a lot of things happened during that time. Following are just a few:

- Whilst on the run, David fled to Ramah for solace with the prophet Samuel.
- He went to Nob to hide out with Abimelech, the priest (1 Samuel 21).
- He went to King Achish of Gath and acted like a madman to gain temporary asylum (1 Samuel 21:10–15).
- He escaped to the cave Adullam, and then the forest of Hareth.
- He was given a chance to retaliate against Saul (1 Samuel 24:1-8).
- He helped out Nabal, got the cold-shoulder treatment, and obtained another wife (1 Samuel 25:1-44).

During his time on the run, David's relationship with the Lord was consistent. Whenever he was in trouble, he called upon the Lord, leaving many of his treasured intimate outpourings that we can read for ourselves today. Although his bond with Michal was strained, he leaned heavily upon the God of Israel.

He also proved himself to be an excellent leader amongst the bevvy of six hundred male companions who followed him. His resilience in those difficult years was extraordinary. God had helped him out of so many difficulties; and his relationship was solidified through his total reliance upon him.

And during those years, something had happened to Michal. David was not there at her side as a protector, husband, or lover, and she did not yet have any babies to look after in his absence. When was her handsome prince ever coming back? She had assisted him in his lowest hour, and he hadn't returned. When she went to bed, he wasn't there beside her. It was always empty. There was nothing romantic going on—no intimacy, and no pillow talk or gestures of love. She probably didn't even feel married any more. She would have felt abandoned and neglected. Not necessarily in that first week, but as the weeks became months and the months became years, the torment of disconnect between the couple eventually revealed itself.

In chapter 25, Saul solved one of the problems called loneliness and passed Michal over for marriage to a man by the name of Phaltiel, son of Lamish. Interestingly, this man was from the tribe of Benjamin, so it only made sense to Saul to keep things in the family. Michal could have resisted and waited for her husband to return, but she didn't. This may have been a cruel gesture from Saul towards David.

These events happened over a span of approximately thirteen years, as David was crowned king over Hebron at the age of thirty. He genuinely lamented over the death of Saul and his best friend, Jonathan. Their lives were so intricately interlinked, and what was most admirable about David was his constant refusal to kill Saul— the Lord's anointed.

Now that David was king, it was time to reclaim those things that had been taken from him, one of them being his former wife. With the assistance of Abner, who now wanted to support the new king, he requested that Michal be sent to him. Ishbosheth—another of Saul's sons—removed her from her husband Phaltiel, who was more besotted with her than she was with him.

The scriptures are silent as to how she responded when she saw David once again. It had been several years since their last reunion, and they would have both changed considerably in appearance. There would also have been spiritual and emotional changes in them.

It is only when we get to chapter 6 of 2 Samuel that we capture the essence of what was really going on with her. Emotionally, she already had to cope with the deaths of her father and her brothers Jonathan, Abinadab, and Malchishua. Now she had to feel the detachment of again being separated from the other husband, who was very reluctant to let go of his proud princess. It is surprising to note that she wasn't the clingy one!

David had never forgotten the kindness and cooperation she had shown in helping him to escape the clutches of her jealous father. Back then, she would've known about the tension inside the palace walls, but she was not probably committed enough to God to step in and do more, as Jonathan had done.

By welcoming Michal back into the household, King David extended to her his hand of peace, love, and acceptance. And it was also a political move to strengthen his claim to the kingdom.

After David's coronation as king in Zion, he was keen to bring back the ark of the covenant to the city. It had been temporarily staying at the house of Obed-Edom for three months. During that time, this man and his family had experienced blessings upon blessings, because the presence of the Lord was there.

It was now time to move the blessings back into the residency of the city and celebrate the ark's return. So one day, David arranged for this to happen with rejoicing and gladness. A procession of people followed him from Obed-Edom's house to Zion, 'with shouting and the sound of the trumpets.' (2 Samuel 6:15). He gave generous offerings of oxen and fatlings—the best sacrifices—filled with plenty of blood.

At this climatic event, David got caught up in the exuberance of praise, dancing with all his might skilfully and passionately before the ark (the presence of the Lord), in the sight of all the people, wearing just a simple linen ephod generally worn by the Levitical priesthood. As he rejoiced, so the people rejoiced in acknowledgement of God's presence and goodness amongst them once again.

Whilst this occurred, princess Michal was looking out of a window, watching him dancing and leaping before the Lord, '… and she despised him in her heart.' (2 Samuel 6:16). She was not part of the spiritual celebrations. She stood apart from them, detached and disinterested in being involved with worshipping God. Instead of supporting and sharing with the crowd and her acquaintances, she stood with aloof indifference. (She had, in effect, closed her heart and mind from receiving from God at the time when everyone else was worshipping and rejoicing.)

As she watched her husband, the various emotions that had remained hidden in the inner recesses of her soul for so long now rose to the surface. Outwardly, her face betrayed her by not showing signs of genuine happiness or joy, but rather the disdain and haughtiness in her eyes, which are the windows of the soul. No longer were her thoughts towards David those of the love, warmth, and admiration that she once possessed, but rather those of tangible hatred. Her love towards him had grown cold.

'For prophecy came not in old time by the will of man: but holy men of God spoke as they were moved by the Holy Ghost' (2 Peter 1:21). There was no way we would know what was in her heart unless we were specifically told. God wanted to let us know, from the holy men who were inspired to write accordingly by the Holy Ghost, that in her heart she had developed hatred towards her husband.

The extent of her disdain was brought to light in the words she spoke to him in verse 20 of 2 Samuel 6. She strolled up to him and said, 'How glorious was the king of Israel today, who uncovered himself today in the eyes of the handmaids of his servants, as one of the vain fellows shamelessly uncovered himself.' Michal had offended the king, who was father to the King of Kings.

Her words were fuelled with some revealing facts about the actual dynamics between her and David's lives.

The statement was loaded with sarcasm and disrespect. Reading between the lines, we can infer that her feelings for him had shifted immensely. She no longer cared about him; neither did she choose to recognize his status as king of Israel. Her words betrayed what she really thought about him. She commented on the way he had behaved in front of the handmaids and accused him of acting like a pathetic lunatic or a vain person, as well as on the way he had danced and pranced about—it just wasn't royal protocol.

The statement also revealed what was in her heart. How it was spoken was not becoming of a princess or of someone who loved her husband. Her words dripped with annoyance as she talked about how glorious he was, and how he was king of Israel. She wouldn't even use his name. If David had been feeling amorous towards her that evening before then, she switched his feelings off with her harsh language. She was more concerned about his behaviour than about the fact that the ark of the covenant was now safely restored in the tabernacle.

David's response to this outburst was remarkable. He said,

'It was before the Lord, who chose me before your father, and before all his house, to appoint me ruler over the people of the Lord, over Israel: therefore will I play before the Lord. And I will yet be more vile than this, and will be base in my own sight; and of the maidservants which you have spoken of, of them shall I be had in honour' (2 Samuel 6:21-22). (This would refer to his other wives and concubines).

Subsequently, Michal was cut off from the rest of his household. She was a wife, but in name only. It is possible that he didn't touch her again. And if he did, God ensured that she never got pregnant. He no longer took her to bed. She was sexually and emotionally deprived of his amorous advances and the affection that she once cherished. She was part of the household but was no longer a part of his life. She had no children with him or for him till the day she died. How tragic.

Michal had allowed the roots of bitterness to bear ugly fruit. Consequently, she blocked any chance of creating life. She had effectively killed her own baby. Built up over time, this hate had transformed into gradual loathing, not the giddy love she once had for him. Beneath those layers were self-belittling, humiliation, passive-aggressiveness, and narcissistic behaviour, which she had entertained.

Her inward emotions of hatred produced other monsters: resentment, bitterness, jealousy, anger, a critical spirit, and pride. God was not prepared to deliver that in human (baby) form with his servant who was 'a man after his own heart'. (1 Samuel 13:14). Ultimately, God saw her heart and her motives and kept her womb closed.

There were women in the Bible who were barren, but through prayer there was deliverance. There was Rachel, Manoah's wife, and Rebecca, to name just a few. We don't hear any mention of Michal praying for a child as the other women did; and we don't know if she ever figured out the reason for her barrenness.

In 2 Samuel 21, there arose a sensitive situation in which blood was demanded. Saul, during his reign, had discriminately and deliberately killed the Gibeonites, a tribe whom the Israelites had vowed never to destroy. As a result of this killing, God sent famine into the land for three years straight. David needed to know how to resolve this, so he asked the Lord. In order to have retribution, David also asked the Gibeonites what he could do. They requested that seven sons (or male grandchildren) of Saul be delivered up and hung upon a hill. In that same chapter, those nameless five boys—the nephews that Michal looked after for Merab, belonging to Saul's family—are also included.

Sometimes we can deprive ourselves of the very blessings we seek, owing to careless words, works, envy, evil, and strife. When we do not confess, we deny ourselves the right to deliver or birth any good thing that may be due to us. Instead we reap the consequences of our treacherous actions. Because of iniquity, the love of many will wax cold. (Matthew 24:12).

In an excerpt from The Relationship Handbook by George and Linda Pransky, regarding *Barriers to Relationship Intimacy*, we can gain further understanding about Michal.

No. 7 – Mockery and devaluation of your partner kills love.

Couples want to be esteemed by each other. There is no excuse whatsoever for diminishing your partner. Mockery and devaluation are inevitably symptoms of anger, resentment, personal insecurity, fear, personal unhappiness, or pathological narcissism. If you feel the urge to put your partner down, refrain from it, and try to find the source of this impulse. This will generally involve some unfinished personal or relationship business. Giving in to the impulse to mock and devalue your partner will eventually cause their love for you to wither away and die.

It is a strange irony that both Saul and Michal once loved and hated David. The change occurred with Saul when David was first introduced as a court musician to drive away the evil spirits that plagued him. And then it happened with Michal, Saul's daughter, who sadly, over time, began to foster negative emotions towards him.

There are lessons that we can learn from Michal's life. We know what the scriptures say with regard to this: 'Wives submit yourselves unto your own husbands' (Ephesians 5:22). And, 'Husbands, love your wives' (Ephesians 5:25).

Love is an investment, but it is not passive. In every marriage, one must be prepared to make a lot of personal and joint sacrifices in order for it to work. Commitment to a lasting relationship requires effort, communication, and lots of emotional energy. It's only what we put into a relationship that we get out of it. It's not enough to just say, 'I love you.'

There will be occasions when you don't feel in love with your spouse. It is then that you need to find and create opportunities to show that you care until your heart is aflame with passion.

Women have a strong communicative repertoire within their reach, and how it is used will fundamentally determine the duration and strength of a relationship. Spoken words have great power; they can uplift or, as in the case of Michal, destroy.

The power of touch is just as important. Left out, it can leave a relationship between couples much like a fridge: emotionally cold on the inside. As humans, we have the capacity to receive and reciprocate loving affection. When we do this in the right way, it has its rewards. Internally, we can emotionally switch off when the wrong words are said or the right touch is inappropriately given at the wrong time.

It cannot be stressed enough that one of the main key aspects for healthy relationships is good communication, which was clearly missing between Michal and David. Additionally, the lengthy duration of David's absence created emotional distancing in Michal. Plus there was a tremendous lack of intimacy and closeness. In a young marriage, these things are crucial building blocks towards a strong foundational relationship.

During his years on the run from Saul, he had no opportunities to run back to the palace to continue his commitment towards his wife, as it was no longer safe for him to remain there.

Today, when mobile phones are aplenty, we are bombarded with numerous methods of communication: emails, texts, shares, photos, Twitter, WhatsApp, Facebook, TikTok, and many other such websites. If David had had a mobile phone, it's very possible that he would have kept in constant contact with her. Alas, such was not the case.

During David's absence, she closed her heart off to him. It was Michal who had lost her first love to David, and in return she ended up alone, bitter, and barren. Besides that, she had also lost respect for him. What came out of her mouth affected her heart, and what came out of her heart affected her words.

David's affections for Michal hadn't died until the moment she spoke the inner utterances of her heart on that celebratory day.

PASSION—MORE THAN A THREE-STOMP APPEAL
(Based on 2 Kings 13)

WHAT DOES PASSION MEAN to you? Does it mean being an artist? Doing something that defies death, such as bungee jumping? Climbing a mountain? Walking over hot coals? Running as an athlete and representing your country? Shouting at your favourite pop star? Supporting a building project? Being a salesperson? Being a dedicated mother? Trainspotting? Being an astronaut? You get the picture.

For starters, passion takes endurance, energy, and lots of focus. It also includes a love and consummate devotion to what you do or become. Added to this concept is concentration: anything worth striving for will always involve a cost or form of sacrifice in terms of commitment, dedication, time, or devotion to any given task, person, or thing. It will take up your time—lots of it. It can take hours, months, or years to achieve an outcome.

Consider, for example, people who study martial arts. They will no doubt familiarize themselves with literature on the topic and watch videos of famous experts, such as Bruce Lee and Jackie Chan, for example. They will attend tournaments and possibly join classes to learn the arts in a more practical way, developing the stages of the different forms and what they represent. They will learn meditation, breathing techniques, the symbolism of movements, and silence through the processes of culture. Hours will be carved out in making an investment that will influence their whole aspect and self-belief.

If passion were a colour, what colour would it be? It would be red, naturally. It was because of passion and determination, mingled with an immense and intense love for humankind, that Jesus came down from heaven and was crucified for our wrongdoings.

Love is a major component of determination when someone says to you, 'I love cooking because ...' or 'I'm passionate about selling because ...' I remember the smells of Mum's cooking that used to waft out of the kitchen and into my nostrils when I was a child; it made me passionate about cooking.

Some other statements you're likely to hear from passionate persons are 'I love the adrenalin rush' and 'I get a buzz from clinching a deal ...'

All this is to highlight a story about a king of Israel named Joash, who makes a brief appearance in 2 Kings 13:14–19.

To unravel the moral of the story, it would be ideal to get an idea of who Joash was and what his character was like.

What do we know about him? His name means 'Jehovah has given.' He began his reign around 800 BC. He has another similar name attached to him: 'Jehoash'. (See 2 Kings 13:10). His father was Jehoahaz, son of Jehu, king of Israel, which comprised the ten northern tribes. Jehoahaz reigned for seventeen years.

Jehoahaz's reign was not commendable. He walked in the sins of Jereboam, who served idols. Because of his disobedience to God, this king was delivered up into the hands of Hazael, king of Syria, and Benhadad as punishment. This same Hazael was anointed king by Elijah. Later, when the king was sick, Hazael went to consult the prophet Elisha concerning his recovery. Elisha told Hazael the king would recover but he would die. He pretended to be surprised by Elisha's statement that he would become king. He returned, suffocated Benhadad, and seized the throne for himself. He reigned for at least forty-three years during the reigns of Ahaziah, Hadadezer, Shalmaneser, and Jehoahaz.

He greatly inflicted punishment upon Israel during Jehu's reign. He took all the territory of the eastern Jordan Valley. Whilst Joash reigned, he captured Gath, threatened Jerusalem, and oppressed Israel all the days of Jehoahaz.

Essentially, Joash had an obvious but great respect for Elisha and was looking for help, as he was aware of his adversary's previous run-ins and victories against his father.

Elisha, although sick and almost ready to die, gave him the opportunity for permanent victory over this enemy of Israel once and for all.

He was given a set of instructions.

1. Take a bow and arrows.
2. Place your hand on the bow.
3. Guide Elisha's hand on the bow.
4. Open the eastern window.
5. Shoot.
6. Declare victory: 'The arrow of the Lord's deliverance, and the arrow of deliverance from Syria: for you shall smite them in Aphek, till you have consumed them' (2 Kings 13:17).
7. Take up the arrows.
8. Smite the ground.

These eight short, straightforward instructions were given by God through his servant Elisha. Up until the seventh code, Joash was a winner and had ticked nearly all the boxes.

Let's explore this a little more regarding our application today.

1. Bows and arrows: The weapons of warfare are not carnal but are made mighty through God. We must use them effectively and coordinate them with faith. Prayer, fasting, and supplication are crucial keys to decisive victory in Christ Jesus. (1 Corinthians 10:4–5). As an external component of faith, David used a simple catapult with five stones to confront Goliath. Joshua used clay jars filled with light and

trumpets to confuse his Midian enemies. Esther used food to lure Hamen out of his deadly trap, and his fate was sealed.

2. Put your hand on the bow: Employ the instruments given. If we fail to utilize the strategies, methods, and plans, then we cannot be guaranteed the success we require.

3. Guide Elisha's hand on the bow: Elisha the elder strengthened his hand to use the bow. It's a good idea to engage someone else to assist you. Timothy instructed Titus, and Aaron and Hur held up Moses's hands during the conquest of the Amalekites. Having someone seasoned in spiritual warfare can give you a triumphant edge.

4. Open the window eastward: The Syrian army was positioned eastward. They had taken Jordan for themselves, but now Joash had the window of opportunity to reclaim and claw back these cities out of the enemies' hands (2 Kings 10:23). When an opportunity presents itself for you to be spiritually secure and victorious, grasp it with both hands.

5. Shoot! Do it. Obedience is better than sacrifice. Remember what happened to King Saul and the Amalekites (1 Samuel 15).

6. Speak words of confidence in your mouth: Say to your soul, 'I can do all things through Christ who strengthens me', 'I shall not die, but live and declare the works of the Lord ...', and 'No weapon formed against me shall prosper ...'

7. Take up the arrows: Retrieve the weapons of victory in your hands. They signify the defeat of your enemies. When we dress ourselves in the armour of God's righteousness, we become invincible, because we have the army of God behind us as well; it is the armour of light conveying truth, salvation, righteousness, faith, his words, and peace. We have powerful pieces of protection from the seen and unseen forces of darkness that may come against the soul.

8. Strike the ground: Whether Joash felt this part of the sequence (the jumping up and down in front of Elisha, who doesn't hint about how many times he should do this) a tad stupid or nonsensical we don't know. He left this to his own

discretion and passion. What we do know is that he gave a half-hearted effort to strike the ground as beneath his demeanour, therefore giving him a partial victory. It was a simple instruction but also an important one. Though he had initially sought the help of a dying prophet, he failed to put in the effort required and to sacrifice the risk of appearing foolish. He could manage only three measly jumps. If he had stomped the ground at least five to seven times, he would have achieved his goal and totally annihilated his adversary. Instead he managed a mere triple defeat.

Let us claim the prize. Stomp like you mean it. Praise the Lord luxuriously and generously. We cannot overpraise God, who is worthy to be praised. David had that kind of mindset, which gave him the God-given description of a man after God's own heart. He put forth exuberant praise, and passion that overflowed at any cost—even ridicule from his own wife—at his own expense.

You have got to really want it. In Matthew 5, the fourth beatitude states, 'Blessed are those who are hungry and thirsty for righteousness: Why?, for they shall be filled.' Isaiah 55:1 echoes the same thought by expressing, 'Ho everyone who thirsts, let him come buy and eat from the (spiritual) waters, buy wine (Holy Spirit) and milk (the word of God), without money and price.' The currency needed is faith and fellowship with God—not money. When we hunger for such things, half-heartedness will disappear, and revelation will appear in no time.

Throughout history, men and women around the world have made remarkable outstanding contributions in the lives of others for society and for themselves. For example, because of a love of medicine and watching her own mother combine special herbs and concoctions, Mary Seacole was instrumental in the recovery and health of many soldiers during the Crimean War, between 1853 and 1856.

In the nineteenth century, Thomas Edison's passion and obsession with electricity and its workings led him to make a succession of electrical products, many of which we still use today. This meant accepting and making errors along the way in order to find the true path to experimentation, correction, and successes.

Athletes have incredible die-hard attitudes which say, 'I can', under every circumstance. In order to win, they cannot entertain the notion of defeat even when outnumbered by persons more than their equal. They fortify their minds, as for them focusing on victory with every determined step, stride, putt, stroke, kick, tackle, or strike as essential for triumph.

Figures like Pete Sampras, Tiger Woods, Serena and Venus Williams, Martina Navratilova, Lewis Hamilton, Sebastian Coe, Stephen Hendry, and Jimmy White have become famous in all fields of sports and other professions. These people have made the necessary sacrifices, have tasted victory, and have been champions more than once.

Let us learn the lessons from Joash's life. When commanded, be obedient; and rather than being passive, be assertive. 'The kingdom of heaven suffers violence, and the violent take it by force' (Matthew 11:12). The righteous are as bold as lions (Proverbs 28:1). Be courageous; be bold. The man Joash was a king, but he exhibited timid tendencies.

Some Other Declarations of Faith

Soul, hope in God, for I shall yet praise him, who is the health of my countenance, and my God. (Psalm 43:5)

I will bless the Lord at all times. (Psalm 34:1)

Fret not yourself of evil-doers. (Psalm 37:1)

He that dwells in the secret place of the most high shall abide under the shadow of the almighty. (Psalm 91:1)

One shall chase 1000, two shall put 10,000 to flight ... (Deuteronomy 32:20)

If we need something, anything ask in Jesus's name. (John 14:14)

When things seem dark—'The Lord is my light and salvation ...' (Psalm 27:1)

(Feel free to add to the list)

THE ACHILLES' HEEL OF KING JEHOSHAPHAT

L ET'S DISCOVER THE MAN made famous in scripture by the name of King Jehoshaphat.

He appears firstly in 1 Kings 22:2 and is present through 2 Kings 3. A brief summary of his life is given in 2 Chronicles 17–21.

Jehoshaphat was the son of Asa, who was a very good and righteous king who reigned for an impressive forty-one glorious years as ruler over Judah. His mother's name was 'Azubah', meaning 'forsaken', and his grandfather's name was 'Shilhi', meaning 'armed'. Jehoshaphat's name means 'Jehovah has judged'.

After his father's death in 870 BC, Jehoshaphat, at the age of thirty-five, became the new king of Judah in 870 BC. His reign overlapped with that of King Ahab, who had reigned three years prior over the Northern Kingdom, which comprised the ten tribes of Israel. During his twenty-five-year reign, Jehoshaphat accomplished many excellent enterprises.

He followed diligently in the steps of his righteous father by removing the high places and groves from out of Judah. He even removed the standing sun images, and heathenistic altars from the high places situated in Judah and Ephraim. He also removed the sodomites from the land.

Just as David had done before him, he diligently sought the Lord (not Baalim), and he was consistent in his relationship with God by keeping his commandments.

Furthermore, in the third year of his reign he sent out five principal men, plus an additional eleven Levite priests throughout the cities of Judah, and established an extensive biblical educational teaching programme from the book of the law. As a result of that, the Word of God was taught thoroughly throughout the land. And because of this, the fear of the Lord was in all the kingdoms of those countries when they heard that the Lord fought against the enemies of Israel. There was peace in these countries because no one wanted to make war with them. Amazing!

He strategically placed many garrisons within the cities of Judah and the land of Ephraim, and he stationed troops in military bases to protect his people. Jehoshaphat built many impressive castles, palaces, and storehouses in the land of Judah. He also had many businesses and had amassed a sizeable number of valiant men ready for war, the total being one million and sixty thousand men who waited on him, prepared for military duty.

God magnified him exceedingly, as he did his father Asa, Uzziah, and Hezekiah. Not only did he make him great, but he also made him extremely wealthy. Judah and the Philistines (who previously had been enemies of Israel) gave him presents. Verse 11 of 2 Chronicles 17 tells us that the Philistines gave a tribute of silver, while the Arabians gave him flocks of seven thousand seven hundred rams and seven thousand seven hundred male goats. That's plenty of money, meat, clothing, and dairy products. This guy had it all simply because he put God first and demonstrated his love into action by removing idolatry from the land, replacing it with the Word of God.

In Israel, on the other hand, the pendulum had swung the other way round. The nation was steeped in paganism because King Ahab had, circa 880 BC, deliberately married a heathen woman who came from Tyre. Her father was a priest-king and had let her loose on promoting her lewd style of religion alongside with her eight hundred and fifty false soothsayers—four hundred for Baal and four hundred and fifty for Asherah, with an intention to infiltrate Israel with it. Ahab, by poor example, encouraged the people to indulge in its evil practices.

Jehoshaphat's Alliance with Ahab

Ahab reigned over Israel for approximately twenty-two years, from around 874 BC to 852 BC. During that time, he made several mistakes, the major ones being his marriage to princess Jezebel, his failure to endorse righteousness in the land, and his worshipping of other idols and engaging in their cultish practices of child sacrifice and temple worship, which involved fornication. He also coveted Naboth's vineyard and conveniently arranged his death, via his wife, so he could secure it. Subsequently, the prophet Elijah foretold of the king's fate, of his household, and of his thoroughly wicked spouse.

In chapter 18 of 2 Chronicles, we are informed that Jehoshaphat joined in a close friendship with Ahab. They were both kings, Ahab ruling in the north and Jehoshaphat in the south. This friendship extended to marital relationships between their sons and daughters, which I will explore later on. Ahab was clearly aware of the king's reputation in Judah and the wealth and honour he had attained during his reign.

One day, near the latter end of his reign, Ahab invited his friend Jehoshaphat and those in attendance with him to a hospitality meal that was served with sheep and oxen in abundance. This meal was intended to persuade the king of Judah to join him in battle at Ramoth-Gilead. Jehoshaphat responded by saying, '[Yes, of course] I am as you are, and my people as your people; my horses as your horses' (1 Kings 22:4).

He further remarked, being a man of God, [Please ask] 'Inquire, I pray thee, at the word from the Lord today!' (1 Kings 22:5). A simple request was made. Ahab was reluctant to utilize a prophet of God. Instead he chose the four hundred prophets of Baal for consultation. In unison they all remarked, 'Go up, for God will deliver it [the battle] into the king's hand' (1 Kings 22:6).

Jehoshaphat was not comfortable about the fact that all four hundred soothsayers spoke in agreement. Not one said no. He asked Ahab whether there was anyone else besides them, and with reluctance Micaiah was called forward. After speaking the same words to appease the king, he was then reprimanded and told to speak the truth instead. What he revealed prepared Ahab to thwart the message which revealed his death. Undeterred, Ahab clad himself to battle in disguise, but he suggested his friend wear his kingly robes for the occasion (which he did)!

Jehoshaphat nearly lost his life in battle, and he would have had not the Lord been on his side when he called on him for help. The thirty-two captains saw a king in robes and presumed it was Ahab. And when they realized it was the wrong man, 'God moved them to depart from him.' (2 Chronicles 18:31) He was later rebuked by the prophet Jehu, who chided him and said,

Should you help the ungodly, and love them that hate the Lord? That is the reason why the wrath of God is come on you. But there are some good things found in you, in that you have taken away the groves out of the land, and prepared your heart to seek God. (2 Chronicles 19:2–4).

'Then we are told that 'a certain man drew a bow at a venture and smote Ahab between the joints of the harness: therefore he (Ahab) said to his chariot man, turn your hand, that you may carry me out of the host; for I am wounded.' (2 Chronicles 1:33).

Evil king Ahab died propped up in his chariot during the battle against the Syrians, and the dogs licked his blood, according to the Word of the Lord.

This is the only account in which we read a story about Ahab and Jehoshaphat supporting each other in this relationship where the good guy almost got killed. But it had even more far-reaching consequences after the death of Ahab.

His Bizarre Relationship with Ahab: What Was the Attraction?

Jehoshaphat was as different from Ahab as night is from day and oil is from water. But whatever the attraction was, during their reigns they became firm, fast friends. As much as they had strengths, they both had weaknesses.

Jehoshaphat was righteous, whilst Ahab was ungodly. And Ahab's character was made much worse by his influential narcissistic wife. It's hard to find or imagine where their commonalities lay, because of their stark differences. That one story alone reveals that Ahab was a devious character who was prepared to let his friend die in battle in order to preserve his own life.

Whilst there are no other stories regarding their friendship, there are further accounts about two of the children they had. This is where the story becomes more complex and intermingled at best, bringing the very worst out of them because of their associations with an evil family.

Familiarity—Family Ties

Clearly, the relationship between Jehoshaphat and Ahab ran very deep, to the extent that in their families they both—coincidentally—happened to have two sons with identical names. Remember: Ahab had seventy sons, but in scripture the focus is on two of them who reigned after their father's death.

Jehoram, son of Jehoshaphat, reigned as king over Judah at the same time that Jehoram, son of Ahab, reigned as king over Israel, though his reign began five years earlier. He was thirty-two years old when he began his reign, which lasted for only eight years. He married Ahab's daughter, Athaliah. Through this union, he followed in the footsteps of his father-in-law, Ahab, and the other kings of Israel, in contrast to his righteous father.

Another atrocious act that he committed was the slaying of his six other biological brothers by fratricide—something Athaliah also engaged in to maintain absolute control of her status as queen over Jerusalem. (See 2 Chronicles 22:10.)

As punishment, God warned him with a letter from Elijah. He had caused the people of Judah to sin and had slain his brothers, who were better than him. Because his ways were displeasing to the Lord, he would be smitten with a great plague that would affect his entire family (children, wives, and possessions). His health would deteriorate, leaving him afflicted with an incurable sickness of the bowels. To top it all off, God would stir up his old rivals, who would take all that he had as spoils, including his sons and wives (except one of his sons), and would leave him with absolutely nothing.

Jehoram, son of Ahab, reigned over Israel in Samaria in the eighteenth year of Jehoshaphat. To summarize his life, this king reigned for a total of twelve years. He was just as bad as his father. However, he at least removed the image of Baal that his father had erected. He got into political hot water because when his father died, King Mesha stopped giving lambs and rams, and rebelled against Israel again. He tried unsuccessfully to regain control of the Moabites, so he approached his father-in-law, Jehoshaphat, for assistance.

Jehoshaphat again happily agreed to help him out, along with the king of Edom. Victory was secured through the intervention of the prophet Elisha, who instructed them on what they needed to do. The prophet even mentioned that had it not been for the fact that Jehoshaphat was there, he would not have regarded Jehoram or helped him out. He was the first of Jehu's victims, and he died from an arrow wound in Jezreel. It was on that occasion that Ahaziah, son of Jehoshaphat, went to visit him.

Another Overlap in the Reigns of Jehoram/Jotham and Ahaziah

It was around that time that God raised another courageous individual named Jehu, who was anointed by an unknown prophet and was specifically hand-picked by God to annihilate the entire family of Ahab, who had been previously cautioned by Elijah after he had seized Naboth's vineyard.

Ahaziah, who was the son of Jehoram, son of Jehoshaphat, was made king by the agreement of the inhabitants of Jerusalem, being the only survivor left of his father's household, who had been slain by the Arabians.

At the age of forty-two, in 841 BC, he became king over Jerusalem, as had his father. His mother was none other than the evil queen-mother Athaliah, the granddaughter of Omri and daughter of Ahab. And as much as he had a righteous grandfather in Jehoshaphat, 'he [decidedly] walked in the ways of the house of Ahab: for his mother was his counsellor to do wickedly' (2 Chronicles 22:3). Subsequently, he did evil in the sight of God like the house of Ahab, as they were his counsellors after the death of his father. His religious policy during his short year indicated his total domination by his mother. He met his death at the hands of Jehu while visiting his uncle Jehoram, who was recovering in Jezreel.

In the meantime, Ahaziah, son and successor of Ahab, reigned for one year in Israel. His name means 'Jehovah has grasped.' He ruled for just two years, and during that time he managed to enlist the services of his father-in-law, King Jehoshaphat, to join him in some shipping ventures.

The verses found in 2 Chronicles 20:35–37 inform us that Jehoshaphat, king of Israel, joined himself with Ahaziah, king of Israel, who was very wicked. He made ships to go to Tarshish, and the ships were made in Ezion-Gaber. 'Then Eliezer the son of Dodavah, prophesied against Jehoshaphat saying, Because you have joined yourself with Ahaziah, the Lord has broken your works. And the ships were broken, that they were not able to go to Tarshish' (2 Chronicles 20:37).

Another version of this account mentions that 'Jehoshaphat made ships of Tarshish to go to Ophir for gold: but they went not for the ships were broken. Then said Ahaziah the son of Ahab unto Jehoshaphat, "Let my servants go with your servant in the ships." But Jehoshaphat would not' (1 Kings 22:48-49).

It would appear that at this stage, the light came on for Jehoshaphat. He finally got the message. Yet again he was ready to help out and join himself again to another evil individual, and God had to send a prophet to get his attention and let him know that he would not be successful with the shipping venture (although it was a good business idea), because of his alliance and connections with Ahaziah (his son-in-law).

When that failed and the ships were broken, Ahaziah still pushed for Jehoshaphat's servants to be involved with his servants instead. But Jehoshaphat did the right thing this time by refusing, as he realized that God was displeased with his associations. This was near the end of his reign, when he was approximately sixty years old.

This same king, Ahaziah, who was heavily influenced by his mother, Jezebel, fell out his upstairs window and became very sick. Subsequently, he sent messages to consult Baalzebub, the god of Ekron, to inquire as to whether he would recover from his disease. Three times Elijah the Tishbite told the messengers, 'Is it not because there is not a God in Israel, that you go to inquire of Baalzebub the god of Ekron? Now then, this is what the Lord says, You shall not come down from that bed on which you are gone up, but shall surely die' (2 Kings 1:3-4). When he realized that the messenger was Elijah, he sent a captain with his fifty to destroy the man of God, who commanded fire to come from heaven and destroy them instead. They failed and he died, according to the Word of the Lord. His son Jehoram, Jehoshaphat's nephew, reigned in his place.

Jehu made a thorough end of destroying Ahab's family. In one day, the rulers of Samaria offered up the seventy heads of King Ahab's sons. So Jehu slew all that remained of the house of Ahab in Jezreel and all his great men, his kinsfolk, and his priests until none remained.

So all Ahab's acquaintances, sons, daughters, friends, and familiar personnel who knew him or were connected to him in some way, his false priests and prophets, and eventually his wife were all obliterated. Why? Because their doctrine had caused an unholy infestation throughout the land of Israel, which in turn caused the people to sin and feel the sting of God's wrath. Their relationships with false idols angered the Lord, and it was time to remove the culprits, who were supposed to be an example to the nation.

Lessons to be Learned

This story needs to be told. Here was a just and godly man called Jehoshaphat, who shared a deep affinity with another Jewish king (Ahab) who got involved with a heathen woman and embraced everything that she was devoted to, including Baal and Ashterah worship. Not only did he tag along with that religious system, but he also caused Israel to follow in the same vein.

1. You can't say yes to everything!

Jehoshaphat was happy to help evil people. When Ahab wanted help, he said, 'Sure.' When Jehoram needed help for war, he said, 'Of course.' When Ahaziah wanted help in shipping, he said, 'Okay, then.' Yet these men were his downfall. In the scriptures, we are told that he joined himself to multiple things.

There is a time and place to defiantly say no, especially if it is inappropriate. Jehoshaphat's friendship with Ahab emerged into further toxic relationships with his sons, his wives, and their families within the family. It would have been much wiser for him to have just walked away and have nothing to do with them, as their lifestyle contradicted his own.

2. Lean not on your own understanding!

Trust in the Lord with all your heart. We can see only the outside of a person, but God looks at the heart (1 Samuel 16:7). Jehoshaphat should have consulted with God regarding whether Ahab was a suitable candidate for friendship or business.

3. You could become subject to abuse, manipulation, and exploitation.

Owing to the nature of their relationship, Jehoshaphat's loyalty extended to the intermarriage between his sons' relationships within Ahab's family. There were interconnections that spilled over into having two of their sons share names, as well as their involvement in war and in the shipping enterprise.

Jehoshaphat's inability to create boundaries within this bizarre relationship led him into numerous troubles. Thank God for the prophets sent into his life to caution him whenever he took a wrong turn! He should have been more wary when Ahab told him to keep his royal robes on when they went out to fight at Ramoth-Gilead. Ahab went out dressed like an ordinary soldier, but that day an arrow struck him by chance, and his fate was sealed.

This king had created security and protection for the country he reigned over, yet he didn't take the trouble to protect his heart. If you fail to establish personal boundaries, you end up becoming vulnerable or exposed to emotional or psychological abuse.

4. Don't be so trusting!

Jehoshaphat was a trusting and loyal individual. He had the right frame of heart to serve the Lord, and he kept his commandments. He was very amenable, agreeable, supportive, and generous, but unfortunately he was so towards the wrong individuals.

The shipping venture with his son-in-law Ahaziah was a wonderful business opportunity to obtain gold from Tarshish. But his relative was an evil man consumed by the ways of his parents in worshipping idols, with no regard for the God of Israel.

God was protecting Jehoshaphat from any possible hidden snares that would have resulted from this business partnership with Ahaziah. Even when he couldn't persuade him, Ahaziah still tried to involve Jehoshaphat's servants instead, which shows the kind of lengths he went to in order to snag him.

Understand that, unfortunately, not everybody is nice and lovely. Be cautious of the friends and associations you keep. If they cause you psychological harm and you discover that their friendship is false, then it's time to let them go.

5. Don't be such a people-pleaser!

People-pleasing is such a dangerous talent! Why? Because you cannot please people all the time, and you do it to your own detriment. It affects not only your self-worth but also your self-confidence. People also use it as a yardstick to measure or gauge personality flaws. If you are not careful, they will exploit your kind-hearted nature and keep you either under their thumbs or wrapped around their little fingers through manipulative means.

The other disadvantage to the art of people-pleasing is that you end up feeling inferior to others. This is unhealthy, because it suggests that you feel less of a person than you really are. You also don't want to upset them by doing or saying the wrong thing, in order to continually win their affections.

Jehoshaphat was willing to assist his friends to the point of endangering himself, without even recognizing or considering the implications of his decisions. By pleasing them in agreement, he displeased God.

There is nothing wrong in helping people; just make sure that the reasons you do so are valid. If what you are doing feels wrong in your conscience or in God's sight, then remove yourself from the situation gracefully.

6. Recognize the difference between tolerance and zero tolerance.

In toxic relationships, generally one individual becomes the giver whilst the other is a taker. One person will tolerate whatever comes his or her way in the name of peace, even when he or she knows that the other person's behaviour is unacceptable. The two may even quarrel about it, but there will be a winner, and it will not necessarily be you.

It then becomes a psychological battle, and in that battle you must decide whether or not this is all there is. Is the other party willing to change, or will you just walk away? Sometimes you've invested so much in the relationship that it seems to be a very difficult decision to make.

When Rose West married Fred West in 1972, she didn't seek to leave or divorce him afterwards once she realized what sort of person he was. Instead she chose to stay with him and became deeply involved and entrenched with his depraved and licentious behaviour.

As the years went by, she not only tolerated this behaviour but also displayed devious and manipulative behaviour similar to her husband's. When the world finally got a glimpse of the murders and atrocities committed inside and outside the home in 1994, it was far too late. The garden and floorboards were dug up, and bodies were found. The police and press, and media worldwide, assembled at Cromwell Street, Gloucester, and both parties were heavily sentenced for the rapes and murders of their victims.

7. You can't change people!

The strangest consequence about this relationship between Jehoshaphat and Ahab is that the latter did not seek to change his lifestyle towards righteousness even though his friend more righteous than he. Neither does it seem that Jehoshaphat tried to encourage him in that way. What could they indeed talk about if the God of Israel was not part of Ahab's equation or thinking?

It is said that holiness doesn't rub off, which is certainly true in this story. All the kings and queens (except Jehoshaphat) who were contemporaries during that time lived ungodly lives and displeased God. They died in terrible circumstances and historically left notorious impressions so that we can learn sobering lessons from them today.

Jehoshaphat didn't seem to question his relationships at all, either. He was all too accepting and willing to partner with his friend Ahab, to the point of losing his life. He was also willing to help his sons-in-law, who were not on the same page with his belief system. It would appear that the soul tie linked them to intermarriage and very little else.

When something is wrong in a relationship, good communication is key to finding resolution. You have the power to either reject or accept bad behaviour. Work things through with better solutions. You have the option to change the situation and work towards a win-win option.

Tolerance is good to an extent, but when it affects the relationship negatively, then it's time to move to zero tolerance.

The four children who shared the names Jehoram and Ahaziah all reigned—and sadly, they were all bad leaders. Two were sons of Ahab, and the other two were sons of Jehoshaphat. And yet the latter rejected God and embraced the pagan influences of their father-in-law, and even worse, one of them married Princess Athaliah, the daughter of Jezebel. Righteousness in parents doesn't always yield righteousness in children, although the pattern is there. Consider Jacob and Esau, and Cain and Abel, for instance.

Why do opposites attract? In reality we tend to gravitate to people who have interests similar to ours or backgrounds similar to ours. We may be opposed in views or values, but generally it's about seeing eye to eye.

In the case of Jehoshaphat and Ahab, their relationship was indeed strange, and behind the scenes Ahab exploited his friend's vulnerabilities of simplicity, openness, and kindness without questioning his strategies (especially in the case of the battle at Ramoth-Gilead) or tolerance of his behaviour, to his own advantage.

The ramifications of this relationship spiralled into their families and their in-laws. It affected their belief system, and that of the country they all reigned over.

Be not unequally yoked together with unbelievers: for what fellowship has righteousness with unrighteousness? And what communion has light with darkness? And what concord has Christ with Belial? Or what part has he that believes with an infidel? And what agreement has the temple of God with idols? For you are the temple of the living God ... (1 Corinthians 6:14–16)

Let us be mindful that, in our relationships with other people, we do not make the same kind of mistakes that Jehoshaphat made, as this could cause us to potentially lose out on the kingdom of God.

THE LEAH SYNDROME: REJECTION AND ACCEPTANCE

L EAH WAS THE OLDER sister of Rachel. Her name means 'weary'. She was an attractive and striking woman, with the kind of eyes that gave her a tired look.

Her father was a duplicitous man named Laban, who was also the brother of Rebecca, who married Isaac and who also bore the children Esau and Jacob.

Her sister Rachel was beautiful and tender-eyed; she was employed as a shepherd and tended their father's sheep.

Jacob, who was on the run from Esau, from whom he had stolen his blessing through trickery, was cautioned by Isaac, his father, not to marry a wife from the Canaanite tribe (as his brother had), but '… to marry from the house of Bethuel, from the daughters of Laban your mother's brother' (Genesis 28:2). He travelled from Canaan to Padan-Aram in Syria, and prior to his encounter with Rachel, he had had a dream about a ladder which extended from heaven to earth, with angels ascending and descending it.

On Jacob's journey, he approached a well in a field and a gathering of three flocks of sheep with their owners. That well watered all those sheep, and a great stone covered the mouth of the well. Rachel was responsible for one of the three flocks, and they would wait together and allow the sheep to drink at the same time before rolling back the stone and dispersing.

On that day, Jacob was available to uncover the well, so the sheep were watered earlier than normal. When he saw Rachel, who was mentioned earlier in conversation between Jacob and some folk, he kissed her and wept. Rachel then ran and told her father about this stranger, who just happened to be a near relation of theirs.

Hospitality was shown towards Jacob from Laban's household. He also negotiated his wages with Laban. They struck a deal, and it was agreed upon that Jacob would work seven years and have Rachel as his wife.

Greedy Laban soon discovered that Jacob had made him a very prosperous man over the several years he had worked for him, and he wasn't prepared to let go of his golden goose, so to speak! So by tricking Jacob into marrying his older daughter, he was forced to work another seven years just to obtain the love of his life—Rachel. Thus Laban was having his cake and eating it too.

As things turned out, Jacob was deceived on his wedding night, and it was only in the morning that he discovered that the wife he had been given was not Rachel but Leah. Can you imagine how disappointed he was at the discovery? It is at this point that we learn that Leah was hated.

Jacob was immediately placed into a polygamous situation. His first and only priority was to marry Rachel and have children with her alone. Leah was forced into marrying Jacob (by her father), causing Jacob's original plan to be changed. But as a result, we also see the beginnings of the fulfilment of the covenantal promise regarding the family of Abraham, who were to be as numerous as the stars of heaven and as the sands of the earth.

Even whilst he was married to Leah, his heart was captivated by her beautiful sister. Despite Jacob's behaviour, Leah maintained incredible resilience and was able to accept herself and keep going, to keep loving, and to keep the relationship alive as much as possible. She refused to let the situation get the better of her. As she poured her heart into her relationship with God, he restored her holistically, enabling her to love herself, her husband, and also her children.

Indeed, she would have had her moments of sadness, tears, and insecurities while locked inside an empty marriage, but she allowed

God to give her the confidence to be a good wife and housekeeper. She probably wasn't privy to any marriage counselling or anyone to mentor her through those lonely years. She had to walk it out day by day, finding a reservoir within her soul of the energy she needed to carry on in her unhappy existence.

We are told that 'when the Lord saw that Leah was hated, he opened her womb' (Genesis 29:31). Rachel, however, was barren. A strange paradox occurred. Clearly Jacob was spending copious amounts of time with Rachel, but they clearly weren't making any babies! And one can only imagine how Leah felt. If the tents were nearby, she might have heard the laughter and merriment she was deprived of.

During that time, Leah was in a relationship that was half-baked. She functioned as a wife and partner, and yet it wasn't paying dividends for her. Jacob was not treating her as his queen or showering her with the kind of affection and attention she justly deserved, as he was Rachel.

To be fair, she was placed in that deceptive position of union because of her selfish father, Laban. It was impossible for her to just walk out of the marriage, because in that culture husbands owned their wives and paid dowries to keep them. Furthermore, for her to walk out from under Jacob's covering would have meant her denying herself the marital benefits of security, protection, and belonging not just for herself but also for the children. To that end, God recognized the mistreatment and rewarded her for her loyalty in the marriage.

The love that she craved from her husband was now being transferred to her children. God ensured that she found her self-worth and appreciation tied up in the eyes of those she nurtured and brought up. They were able to give her a facet of the love and appreciation she sought, to help banish the seeds of rejection and abandonment.

Her ego may have felt bruised, and she may have felt rejected, cheated, unsexy, unattractive, unnoticed, unappreciated, unloved, ignored, unwanted, worthless, and insecure. Although she was unloved by Jacob, Leah was able to find true and lasting love through

God. She took her tears and frustrations to God, who enabled her to endure a relationship that was bereft of genuine love. Leah had a marital relationship with God instead, and as a result he healed her sexually, emotionally, psychologically, and spiritually.

Let's take a look at the names of the children she gave birth to in much closer detail. Leah had six children: five boys and one girl, plus two other sons from her handmaid, Zilpah.

'Reuben' means 'see a son'. 'Surely the Lord has looked upon my affliction; now my husband will love me' (Genesis 29:32). Leah could be expressing here, 'If you won't look at me …' 'If you won't pay attention to me when I look at you …', 'If you won't look me in the eyes and tell me that you love me … then look at your son that we've made together', 'Look at his fingers and toes', or 'Look at him.'

'Simeon' means 'who hears.' 'God has heard that I was hated' (Genesis 29:33). For her second son, she could be saying, 'If you won't acknowledge me or take any notice of me …', 'If you won't listen to me when I talk to you …', 'If you won't pay any interest in me as an individual …', or 'Then listen to your son, listen to his cries … he is *our* son from *my* womb.'

'Levi' means 'joined'. 'Now this time my husband will be joined to me because I have borne him three sons' (Genesis 29:34). Here she is saying, 'Jacob, I've given you a family of boys. You are my husband and I love you. In our brief union we are joined together by Levi.'

'Judah' means 'praise the Lord.' Her fourth son was conceived in quick succession, and then she left off childbearing. Here she is saying, 'Jacob, look at your son! He is the one that will cause praise within the family. He is special. Pay attention, because one day Someone great will come from his lineage! I have so much to give God thanks for.' This child's entrance into the world was truly vital to the introduction of the royal dynastic lineage from which David and Jesus would ultimately come. As for Leah, to give birth to this son was a wonderful blessing bestowed upon her, especially as the wife that was initially ignored.

One day, young Reuben plucked some mandrakes whilst in the field. Rachel asked her sister for them with a view to aid her fertility.

These mandrakes were potent plants with roots that resembled the arms and legs of humans, and mandrake was known to aid with fertility. Conjugal arrangements were negotiated, and Leah was able to secure the evening with Jacob. Imagine Rachel's shock at discovering that Leah was expecting again. Sadly for Rachel, the fertility-enhancing plants didn't work as she had expected.

'Issachar' means 'hired' or 'reward'. Here she says, 'Husband, here is your next son that God has given us. I've had to earn my reward by asking my sister's permission to have you all for myself for the night, for the sake of my son Reuben's mandrakes.'

Leah was able to claim bragging rights for having spent the entire evening alone with Jacob, and there was nothing he could do about it. As for Rachel, she was becoming increasingly jealous of the fact that her sister was having children whilst she was having difficulty conceiving. She was so desperate and was now having to emotionally deal with this gynaecological minefield of trying to conceive. Although she was so secure and contented in her relationship with Jacob, her desire to bear children was driving her insane—closer to suicidal—in an effort to give him something that resembled their love for each other. In her frustration, she began to quarrel with her husband about the dilemma.

Prior to taking the mandrakes, Rachel decided to introduce her handmaid, Bilhah, into the marriage in order to secure children by her. As a result, Dan and Naphtali were produced. Their names meant 'Judgings' and 'wrestling with God', respectively. However, she still yearned to have children of her own, which she eventually did. God opened her womb, and she produced two boys, one called 'Joseph', which means, 'to add', and one called 'Benjamin', meaning 'Son of my right'. She exclaimed, 'God has taken away my reproach and will give me another son!'(Genesis 30:23-24).

Leah, in turn, gave her handmaid, Zilpah, to Jacob. Zilpah produced a further two boys to the ever-increasing brood: Gad and Asher, whose names mean 'a troop' and 'happy', respectively.

With the name 'Gad', Leah may have been saying, 'Look, Jacob,

Gad is part of a growing troop of children. These are your sons. Now you will accept me not just as a mother but also as your wife.'

'Zebulon' means 'dwelling.' Here Leah may have been saying, 'God has given me a good dowry; now my husband will live with me because I have borne him six sons.'

Dinah was Leah's daughter, whose name meant 'judgement'. By this Leah may have been saying, 'God has judged this situation and has dealt with it equally and fairly.'

In Deuteronomy chapter 21, verses 15–17, the Lord informs Moses to advise husbands of what would happen if they were to show preferential love to one wife over the other.

If a man has two wives, one beloved, and another hated, and they have born him children, both the beloved and the hated; and if the firstborn son be hers that was hated: Then it shall be, when he makes his sons to inherit that which he has, that he may not make the son of the beloved firstborn before the son of the hated, which is indeed the firstborn: but he shall acknowledge the son of the hated for the firstborn, by giving him a double portion of all that he has: for he is the beginning of his strength; the right of the firstborn is his.

As we delve further into the lives of the children and wives, we discover that the love/hate relationships with the once hated wife extended towards her children's attitudes towards the beloved son, Joseph, by the favourite wife, Rachel, and their interactions towards him. Jacob began to show preferential love in front of the other brothers, which in turn created envy and caused tensions to fester amongst them so much that they wanted to kill him.

In this story, Leah was the very epitome of rejection. There was nothing physically wrong with her; it was just that Jacob was initially attracted to Rachel and no one else. Leah was unloved by her husband for many years, but she withstood it and bore it patiently when she could have walked away.

As human individuals, we have all in some form or another experienced rejection, but we don't necessarily like to admit to or talk about it. It's like an emotional sting to the soul and a bruise to our self-esteem. Rejection, like harmful words, hurts the soul. If a person gets a cut in is or her skin and experiences bleeding, the individual knows that there will be pain also, depending on the severity of the wound, and the body marvellously responds to heal the injury. If we do not hand it over to God, rejection can bear bitter fruit in response to the situation. Psychologically, it can either harden us, making us mistrusting, or cause us to seek isolation and distance from other people. Conversely, it can draw us closer to God through talking to him and sharing everything that we go through, whether good or bad.

We have all had to deal with rejection in various ways. For instance, when we go shopping, we are making choices regarding acceptance and refusal all the time. We pick products worthy to come home with us, and in those choices we decide why we want something or why we don't. It's a matter of individual preferences and taste. It's also personal to our characters and personalities; no one gets hurt. When we go to school, we choose the kind of friends that we want to hang out with, whether they are good or bad influences on us.

But when it comes to meaningful relationships, it's a very different matter entirely. When it comes to matters of the heart, especially when we are choosing our potential life partners, we need to feel some kind of connection or bonding that attracts us to another person. It can be instantaneous, or it may take time to develop into something special. We may accept someone because he or she is tall, or reject someone because he or she reminds us of someone we were traumatized by.

Like Leah, we were cast off and left to our own devices. Out of decency and concern someone loves us, lifts us up, and gives us worth, self-esteem, and dignity. He loves us unconditionally, warts and all. Though our emotions are trampled on, despised, and oppressed, Jesus died whilst we were yet sinners. He removed our shame and reproach and wiped our sinful slates clean.

He allows us to draw as near to him as moths to a flame, but without being burnt. Through a deeper relationship, we can experience a mature life of commitment, trust, and belonging once again. In our shame, the Lord will emotionally heal us inside and out.

Jesus also experienced rejection during his time on earth. Judas was with him for three and a half years, and at the last hurdle he betrayed his master. Peter, one of his inner-circle friends, denied him in his darkest hour. He was amongst the elders—the scribes and Pharisees, who, because of their envy towards him, tried to trap him in his words. Many times they criticized and challenged him from the Torah, which they scrupulously observed.

With regard to Rachel, she is the very epitome of acceptance in this story. Jacob loved her thoroughly, and she didn't have to struggle to get his attention. He loved her unconditionally, which enabled her to feel loved, contented, and special, with the knowledge that she belonged to someone. She had his heart, and he had hers.

The pyramid of Maslow's theory underscores the message that mankind has needs. There are physiological needs (food, water, warmth, and rest), safety needs (security and safety, belonging), love needs (intimate relationships and friends), esteem needs (prestige and feelings of accomplishment), and, finally, self-actualization needs (self-fulfilment, which covers achieving one's full potential, including creative activities).

Within that pyramid, love and acceptance are centrally placed. So to be rejected damages our self-image and pride; and it can create doubt, depression, hopelessness, and anxiety about one's identity.

We are created to give and reciprocate love and to express care and belonging. This comes from God, who reminds us to love our neighbour as we love ourselves. Sometimes it can take a lifetime for you to accept your own personhood and be happy in your own skin, without anyone having to necessarily validate you as the wonderful human being that you know you are. One small exercise I have personally learned to do is to talk to the mirror and say to myself, 'I am beautiful. I am fearfully and wonderfully made. I am redeemed. I am unconditionally loved by God.' Just making those small, powerful statements from the scriptures can make such a difference to your day, especially if someone gives you a hard time with your self-worth.

In the end, Rachel died during childbirth, so the very person Jacob loved, he couldn't keep forever. Leah was now no longer the second option. Not only did she outlive her sister, but she also shared the family cave in Machpelah, which housed Abraham and Sarah, Isaac, and Rebecca, as well as Jacob.

When we are married to God, he commits himself to us throughout every circumstance. He will not leave or forsake us. He loves and accepts us, warts and all. We can be assured of his ever-abiding presence regardless of where we are. Just as in wedding vows, he promises to take us to have and to hold, to love and cherish, for better or worse, for richer or poorer, in sickness and in health.

Let us remember that we are unconditionally accepted by God. He will reject only those who reject his Son at his Second Coming.

THE LIFE AND TIMES OF JOAB, SON OF ZERUIAH

JOAB WAS A CONTEMPORARY of King David, the prophet Nathan, Absalom, Saul, Adonijah, Abner, Jonathan, and Bathsheba. He was one of three brothers (the other two being Abishai and Asahel), the son of Zeruiah, David's sister.

His name means 'God, his father'. He first appears in scripture in 2 Samuel 2 as the nephew of King David, son of Jesse (see 1 Chronicles 2:15–16).

Joab's name crops up around ninety-one times throughout the two books of Samuel to 1 Kings 2 in the King James Version. He was an unpopular individual and is not often mentioned in church sermons, even though his life coincided with David's own. He was a somewhat violent man, with a tendency to use the sword more than his mouth. Having said that, there are some lessons—negative and positive—that we can learn from his life.

Below is a chart listing some of his traits. As you can see, he wasn't an individual that one would be wise to mess around with. There are a lot of strong characteristics on the chart that highlight his qualities that were well-suited for the military and secret service.

List of Joab's Personality Traits

Assertive	Dominant	Prominent	Wise
Astute	Efficient	Responsible	
Aware	Extroverted	Ruthless	
Bold	Impetuous	Shrewd	
Brave	Impulsive	Sensitive	
Careful	Independent	Sober	
Chloric	Intelligent	Strategic	
Confident	Intuitive	Strong	
Courageous	Loyal	Tenacious	
Cruel	Methodical	Tough	
Decisive	Optimistic	Vengeful	
Determined	Organised	Vigilant	
Devious	Perceptive	Violent	
Diplomatic	Precise	Warrior-like	
Disciplined	Private	Watchful	

Occupation: Commander-in Chief of the Armies of Israel

Second Samuel 2:21–28 demonstrates the sort of ruthless and revengeful streak that Joab possessed. He and his brother Abishai killed Abner in cold blood in retaliation for killing their youngest innocent brother Asaphel, who was known in the scriptures as being swift and as light-footed as a roe. He was so upset and angry about his untimely death that he and his men walked approximately thirteen miles all night to the land of Ma-ha-naim, arriving at Hebron by dawn. He buried his brother in his father's sepulchre in Bethlehem. Bearing in mind that they were not on horseback, they showed great resilience, intrepid determination, disciplined minds, and true grit.

David's comments to and regarding him seemed to fall on deaf ears. Concerning Joab's attitude to the unjust bloodshed on at least two occasions, he would often state, '… the sons of Zeruiah are too hard for me …' You see, whilst David would pause and show mercy, his nephew Joab was not hesitant to use the sword with no regard for those he offended along the way.

In 2 Samuel 8:16, Joab was promoted to a high officer rank; he was made commander-in-chief over the host of David's entire army. He had the well-earned credentials and fulfilled the criteria of a hardened, experienced man of war who had achieved multiple triumphs.

In 2 Samuel chapter 10, David sends his captain out against Hanun, son of Nahash, who had previously shown kindness to him and the children of Ammon. The reason for this was their disrespect and attitude towards David's servants. They accused them of spying with a view to destroying their city. Enter Joab.

Verses 7–14 of 2 Samuel 10 highlights Joab's incredible courage alongside his brother Abishai, even when the odds were stacked up against them. They were sandwiched between the army of the Ammonites and the Syrians; right in the middle of the battle (2 Samuel 10:9) and prepared to fight anyway. He encouraged his brother by essentially saying, 'You cover my back, and I'll cover yours.' The end result was fantastic.

'And Joab drew nigh, and the people that were with him, unto the battle against the Syrians: and they fled before him. And when the children of Ammon saw that the Syrians fled, they also fled from before Abishai, and entered into the city. So Joab returned from the children of Ammon, and came to Jerusalem.' (2 Samuel 10:13–14)

Let this verse challenge us to learn to 'lose our life' and die to selfish ambitions or motives and move out into the unknown, outside our comfort zones. Joab was happy to turn things around to his advantage instead of being intimidated by the circumstances and running away.

Joab dared to stare death in the face and stood defiantly to meet his opponents head on. He confidently spoke words of faith: 'Be of good courage, let us play the men for our people, and for the cities of our God, and the Lord do which seems him good' (2 Samuel 10:12).

He uses the words 'our God', which suggests that he embraced the God of Israel. He wasn't afraid. He was prepared to take calculated risks at the cost of his own life.

Chapter 11: David and Bathsheba: Joab the Go-Between

The infamous chapter in David's life that connected him with his adulterous affair with his mistress Bathsheba - wife of Uriah - and the pre-meditated arrangement of the murder of her husband. Ironically, whilst Joab was instrumental in 'fixing' the death set-up during battle—strategically, David was ultimately guilty of orchestrating the crime, because he needed to cover up the 'pregnancy' of his sins. Joab was just obeying an order. No doubt he was privy to this delicate controversy, but nonetheless with military precision, and upon David's word executed Uriah, by placing him in the hottest part of the battlefront where he tragically died.

Speaking of military matters and tactics, Joab was a diplomatic man who knew just what to say and when to say it. Just check out verses 18–25.

Chapter 12, Verses 26–31: The Outspoken Nature of Joab

On a military expedition, he fought against the city of Rabbah and won it outright. He sent a message to David that he had captured the city of waters. He was to take possession of it or else he would retrieve it and name it after himself. Was that a threat? He was being serious here. He was happy for David to take the credit for this even though he had done this himself. And yet he was also prepared to take the credit had David refused.

His loyalty towards David was unwavering. Clearly he would have admired his leadership and prowess especially in his earlier years, when he was initially introduced to war by cutting off the head of the giant, which nobody else in the army wanted to do. Joab was more mature and was older and wiser than David in military matters and encouraged him whenever possible, as his right-hand man.

Note that he took the crown from the dead king's head, placed it on David's head, and took many spoils. It was also to Joab's credit that he allowed David to obtain something that he had singularly gained. He had great respect for David.

Chapter 14: The Widow of Tekoa and Joab the Peacemaker

Joab's name runs through 2 Samuel 14 like water. He understood that at some point David was pining for his favourite son, who had gone into hiding away from his dad, whom he despised especially because he did nothing to prevent his arrogant half-brother Amnon from raping his beautiful sister Tamar, or to punish Amnon after the deed. It is possible that David would mention his name to Joab during their many conversations, or maybe he just had that kind of faraway look in his eyes that caught his attention.

Without David's knowledge, Joab sought the help of a nameless widow who lived in the area of Tekoa, a small town about six miles from Bethlehem. How he found her, and why he located her, of all widows, will forever remain a mystery. He advised her on how to address the king, what to say to him, and the order of such speech. In essence, Joab, in a subtle way, was trying to establish (and win back) his trust with David through this discourse and, in effect, kill two birds with one stone.

The dialogue between the king and the widow was rather endearing, and although David didn't originally understand the first portion of the conversation (vv. 4–8), he later twigged on to the underlying message when the widow spoke in third person (vv. 13–17).

David was also able to establish that the intellectual speech came from Joab. He knew him well enough to produce a cause as sensitive as that. Joab didn't have to involve himself in the father–son relationship. After all, it was Absalom who killed his own brother in revenge.

Joab was so happy that the king was ready to receive Absalom again that he personally rode all the way to Geshur to fetch him. However, David still would not meet with him. After two years, Absalom got irritable and itchy to move away again. Eventually a reunion ensued, but Absalom was still resentful about his dad's lack of authority regarding his sister Tamar, resulting in the most tragic circumstances.

Chapter 18: Joab as a Ruthless Individual

Within 2 Samuel 14–17, we discover that Absalom caused a revolt and rebellion against his father, David. The children of Israel sided with him to be the replacement king, and David was on the run for his life. Joab knew that David's heart was towards Absalom (who was probably a reminder of himself, as Absalom was handsome).

Chapter 18 follows Absalom's sad demise and death at the hands of Joab. Why? I don't know for certain. But after all that trouble to reunite him with his dad, using the widow as the go-between really took the biscuit. So Joab had the privilege of throwing three darts into Absalom's heart as he dangled suspended between heaven and earth with his long hair caught up in the branches of a great oak tree.

Whether Joab had time to settle into marriage is not discussed. He seemed to be dedicated to his main role in life—fighting. Scripture does not seem to hint at him being married or having any children. However, he was made fully aware that Absalom's life should be spared at all costs. Joab was prepared to pay one man ten shekels of silver and a girdle just to kill Absalom. The wise man's reply was astounding. Absalom's body was abused, hurled into a huge pit in the forest, and covered over with stones, and the people of Israel who had once supported him scarpered home scared.

In verses 19–33 in particular, we observe that Joab really knew how to influence people with choice words. Ahimaaz, the good news carrier, was urged not to run and inform David of his son's death, but the carrier insisted until Joab relented. In the meantime, Cushi was selected to relate. When David finally discovered the truth, he lamented inconsolably over him.

Chapter 19: Advisor and Commander

David was mourning over his son's death. He was now also aware of the culprit guilty of slaying him against his wishes. He had not returned to Jerusalem, but Joab advised him on his behaviour and the effect it had had upon the nation, who looked up to him. In addition to this, he needed to comfort and appease his people, making plans to move back to his palace in Jerusalem in peace immediately.

Chapter 20: Cold–Blooded and Ruthless

Joab strikes with his sword again, this time against Amasa in cold blood. Sheba was a usurper and was drawing people away along with Amasa, his right-hand man—against King David. Sheba was a Benjamite who decided that he no longer wanted to support David's kingship. He announced this with a trumpet. When David asked Amasa to assemble the tribe of Judah, he took longer than the three days required to obey the order. During the revolt, all the Israelites except the tribe of Judah followed this deluded man. Sheba, the instigator, was repeating history again just as Absalom had previously done before him.

Enter Joab. He gathered to himself the Cherethites, and Pelethites—mighty men of war to come out against Sheba to destroy. These two armies together formed as part of David's private bodyguards under the command of Benaiah, the son of Jehoiada, who was especially loyal to him during the rebellions of Absalom and Sheba.

When they arrived in Gibeon, they encountered Amasa. Joab feigned good greetings with his sword concealed under his garment. Amasa met a brutal end.

'... And Joab took Amasa by the beard with the right hand to kiss him. But Amasa took no heed to the sword that was in Joab's hand: so he smite him in the fifth rib and shed out his bowels to the ground, and struck him not again; and he died. So Joab and Abishai, his brother, pursued after Sheba the son of Bichri.' (2 Samuel 20:9-19).

Joab was like your modern-day Terminator! He was relentless in his pursuit of destroying anyone who got in his way, especially with regard to defending the king's honour. In this story, he was after both Sheba and Amasa.

And one of Joab's men stood by him, and said, He that favours Joab, and he that is for David, let him go after Joab. And Amasa wallowed in blood in the midst of the highway. And when the man saw that all the people stood still, he removed Amasa out of the highway into the field, and cast a cloth upon him, when he saw that everyone that came by him stood still. When he was removed out of the highway, all the people went on after Joab, to pursue after Sheba the son of Bichri. (2 Samuel 20:11-13).

This was a truly gruesome and bloody episode. Joab killed to protect King David's honour and his kingdom, stamping out any residue of any traitors in the land. As the day progressed, Joab went throughout the land gathering even more people to get Sheba (a man of Belial—a very wicked person). They ended up in the small city of Abel. Whilst the man was in the city, Joab was prepared to destroy the entire city for that one man. In response to his request, the victory belonged to a people who teamed together, cut off his head, and threw it over the city wall. Joab then retreated with the rest of the people who followed him.

Chapter 24: Numbering the People

Satan provoked David to number the people of God: Judah and Israel. Joab was well aware of the fact that God had promised that his people would be as numerous as the stars of heaven and the dust of the earth—that is, innumerable. He was not keen on carrying out this particular order either. Counting them would be an insult to God. He wisely and gently counselled David against the task, but David's words prevailed. This led Joab on a nine-month-and-twenty-day campaign compiling the census.

Israel accounted for eight hundred thousand men, and Judah five hundred thousand men. This was besides women, children, and the Levites, who served in the tabernacle ministration. When Joab returned with the figures, David's conscience kicked in and he confessed his sin to God. It was such a serious offence. In fact, it was so bad a sin in God's eyes that on this occasion David had to choose his punishment from God.

1 Kings 1: Loyalty Switches

David was now an old and fragile king, and Joab, up until that time, had been a most loyal and faithful servant to him. Joab was also an old man in his mid-seventies. The king had matters to pursue relating to the preparations for installing the next heir to the throne. His firstborn, Amnon, was already dead, and Absalom, who had already revolted against David for the throne, was no longer on the scene. Solomon was God's clear choice and had foretold that this young man would also build his temple. Solomon didn't fill Joab's eye; he possibly viewed him as too peaceful a lad.

Adonijah, another of David's sons, was another suitable prince as king in the wings, but he wasn't God's option. With Joab's help, he tried to wrest the kingdom out of Solomon's hands twice by trying to self-promote himself as king, with a small following of fifty men and chariots, the priest Abiathar in tow.

The event went down like a lead balloon. The court was soon informed when the mighty men of David and Zadok the priest found out that they were not invited to the party. Nathan then informed Bathsheba, who had the king's ear, who ensured them that the pre-celebrations were ended. He then tried again to secure the kingdom, this time by begging Bathsheba's permission to marry Abishag, the beautiful damsel who had once ministered to the king.

David also advised Solomon to use wisdom in dealing with Joab. He died clutching the horns of the altar in the temple, slain for the vicious and unwarranted bloodshed he'd carried out, especially towards the three individuals Abner, Amasa, and Absalom.

Joab had a very strong personality and played a significant role in the life of David. They were both warriors and had few things in common. But in the end, he engaged in a lot of unnecessary slaughter, particularly when he was rattled. He paid a huge price for that. Despite his many faults, (he was far from perfect), on closer examination, there were some glimpses of hope where his character did shine through. He was a courageous warrior who was focused on his role in the army. We can certainly learn from that aspect.

In verse 8 of 1 Chronicles 19, we find the story of Joab being surrounded by the armies of Mesopotamia, Syria, and Zobah.

Let us be continually encouraged by these seven recommendations:

1. Never give up if you are right.
2. Believe that all things work together for good if you just persevere.
3. Don't let the odds discourage you; God is much bigger than all of them.
4. Never let anyone intimidate you or deter you from your goals.
5. Fight, and overcome every limitation.
6. Remember: every winner has dealt with defeat and adversity in life.
7. Try again and again, for in God's strength you'll surely succeed. According to a fourteenth-century story by the

emperor Tamerlane, it took seventy attempts for an ant to push a kernel of maize over a wall.

We can further obtain some more military truths from Joab. Because we are engaged in a spiritual battle, as children of God we must remain focused and keep our wits about us; we must not leave them at the door. There will be battles where we must only 'be still, and know that He is God'.

One Old Testament king in scripture proclaimed a fast and was instructed to 'stand still and see the salvation of God.' In verses 21–22 of 2 Chronicles 20, we are told that

... when he (Jehoshaphat) had consulted with the people, he appointed singers unto the Lord, and that they praise the beauty of his holiness, as they went out before the army, and to say, Praise the Lord; for his mercy endures forever. And when they began to sing and praise, the Lord set ambushment against the children of Ammon, Moab and mount Seir.

This tells us that some battles require worship from a stance of victory—not defeat. When we follow God's battle plan, we can be assured of total triumph, whether that war is coming from inside the marital home, the workplace, school, or even within the church environment.

When we enlist in the battle of life, there will always be something to kill off. We are to die to self-gratification and sin in order to live a life of righteousness against the works of the flesh, which war against the soul, in order that the Spirit can have full control in our lives.

In Galatians 5:16–18, we are advised to,

Walk in the Spirit, and you shall not fulfil the lusts or desires of the flesh. For the flesh lusts against the Spirit and the Spirit against the flesh: and these are contrary the one to the other: so that you cannot do the things that you would. But if you be led by the Spirit, you are not under the law.

These are our personal battles that we must contend with on a daily basis.

Colossians 3:4 tells us to 'Mortify: (put to death/kill) your members which are on the earth: fornication, uncleanness, inordinate affection, evil concupiscence, and coveteousness, which is idolatry.' Galatians 5:17–21 lists even more traits which need to be terminated from within.

There will be temptations that will confront us as hurdles in our way to distract us or take us out. We know from the scriptures that they will come in our direction, but we have many resources at our disposal. Satan and his agents will do all they can in order to get us to displease God, who hates wickedness. In the Bible, there are individuals who faced impulses to do something against their better judgement but who gained the victory over sin. Others caved in and didn't seek repentance, such as Solomon, Judas Iscariot, and Ananias and Sapphira. Daily we must pray to God to 'Lead us not into temptation, but deliver us from evil …' (Matthew 6:13)

These evils will destroy the soul and send us to hell if we do not repent. The Holy Spirit cannot abide in a temple that is crowded with sins that desecrate us and attract demons. This is why we must daily pray for the cleansing blood of Jesus to kill off anything in our lives that could become a hindrance to God using us to bring glory to his Son's name.

In Revelation 21, there is a small list of sins which, if found in our lives, will bar our entrance to the kingdom of heaven. The fearful, unbelieving, and abominable, and the murderers, whoremongers, sorcerers, idolaters, and all liars shall have their parts in the lake which burns with brimstone and fire.

As soon as we accept Christ as Lord and Saviour, we automatically join the spiritual war between good and evil—God and the devil. Ever since the dawn of time in the garden of Eden, the war has been on, and it will continue until Christ's return. In the meantime, let us endure hardship as good soldiers of Jesus Christ. 'No man ([individual] that engages in war entangled himself with the affairs of this life; that he may please him who has chosen him to be a soldier' (2 Timothy 2:3–4).

THE MAN OF GADARENES

IN THE GOSPEL OF Mark, chapter 5, we are introduced to the story of the man possessed by many devils. It can also be found in Matthew 8:28–34 and Luke 8:26–40.

Matthew's version is very succinct in nature, whilst Mark captures the story to the audience he's speaking to and adds more flesh to the narrative. Luke, on the other hand, gives a meticulous and more detailed account of his findings.

After Jesus calmed the raging sea whilst standing in a boat, he and his disciples arrived on dry land in a placed called Gadarenes, a country south-east of the sea of Galilee. Interestingly, the word 'Gadarenes' means, 'those who come from pilgrimage or fight.'

The disciples encountered a man who had multiple devils residing in him for, according to Luke, 'a long time', which could suggest years as opposed to weeks and months. Luke also picked up on the facts that this man wore no clothes and had no permanent place to live in; he dwelt amongst the tombs. This man was so fierce and aggressive that no man dared to come near to him. This possessed man had often been chained, but not for long, as he would soon break free from them, and he was wild. He was unnaturally strong, and what he did was beyond human behaviour. He roamed in the wilderness, tombs, and mountains night and day, crying for help and cutting himself with stones.

This was a very serious affliction. Here was a man who was unsettled; the demons within him made him restless, suicidal, distressed, and strong, but fearful of life. So his only association was tied to death.

The inhabitants of Gadarenes were afraid of this man. His demeanour, state of mind, and presence both frightened them and prevented them from approaching him or from being acquainted with him. They would have been familiar with his upbringing and his family in the neighbourhood. But as time went by, his transformation turned the people away, and they became estranged from him. He did not start his life like that, but at some point of his existence, something went horribly wrong, and instead of getting better, he had gotten worse. No therapist, no doctor, no physician of psychiatry, and no prescribed medicines had been able to cure or heal this man. This was a matter that only Jesus could handle.

It would also seem apparent that the possessed man also symbolized the people of Gadarenes, based upon a few findings.

- Whatever had tormented the man had tormented the people also.
- When Jesus cast out the unclean spirits, the demons earnestly begged that they wouldn't be sent out of the country. In other words, the activities the people were indulging in were attracting the devils to remain within the region and claim it. Luke suggests in his gospel that the devils didn't want to leave at all or go back to hell. They wanted to inhabit someone or something.
- Matthew 12:43–45 tells us that when the unclean spirit is gone out of a man he walks through dry places, seeking rest and finds none. Then he says, I will return into my house from whence I came out, and when he comes he finds it 'empty', swept and garnished (decorated). Then he goes and taken with himself 7 other spirits more wicked than himself, and they enter and dwell there, and the last state of that man is more worst than the first.
- If we entertain or succumb to the demonic delights of the adversary, we give sway to his hold on us and create a

stronghold, making it more difficult to give up on those things which could potentially destroy us.

When asked its name, the reply it gave was 'Legion, for we are many' (Mark 5:9). Evil attracts evil, like carrion to dead meat and flies to faeces.

This nameless man was somebody's son, somebody's husband, somebody's nephew, somebody's friend. And whatever had happened in his life had also attracted demons. He may have experienced emotional and psychological pain or some kind of trauma. Certain emotions do not travel alone. Whatever the problem, the thing that had occurred in his life had prised opened a door. Such problems come dressed as pain, anguish, fear, wrath, trauma, suicide, drug abuse, drug misuse, sexual promiscuity, self-harm, low self-esteem, depression, stress, post-traumatic stress disorder, psychological dysfunction of the mind, and multiple personality disorder. In fact, the list is endless. Just one element alone can have so many attachments added to it. Demons do not tend to enter as a single agent. As the scripture asserts, when the house is empty, they bring other demons along in order to control and ultimately to destroy the host.

In the Roman military, a legion consisted of a captain who was in charge of five thousand soldiers. So given the fact that two thousand demons were cast out of this man, certainly implies the serious extent of his fragile state of mind and his health.

Verses 11–13 reveal some interesting insights within the scriptures. 'Now there was nearby on the mountains a great herd of swine feeding.' How come the pigs were being sustained, and so many of them? Why not cattle, sheep, and goats?

Pigs are symbolic of all things unclean, including covetousness, gluttony, and lack of self-control. People were feeding these pigs and were quite content to do so. In the spiritual realm, we are cautioned 'not to cast pearls before swine' (Matthew 7:6). We are to depart from iniquity, cleanse our hearts from evil, and so forth. Yet the swine herdsmen were happily feeding uncleanness with uncleanness; this is one possible clue as to why the devils didn't want to leave the country.

Jesus would not allow the devils to enter the people he came to save, but by express permission, he allowed the devils to enter the pigs instead. What a picture! The many multiple spirits that had such an unholy grip on the man were now causing havoc among the two thousand or so pigs, who hurtled headlong into the sea below. The unclean spirits entered the unclean, accessible pigs, who fortunately didn't survive the transformation of their fate.

Those who fed the pigs ran away in fear and panic, not in delight or pleasure that the man they had once known as possessed was now free from oppression. And in one brief moment, he was transformed from a restless, naked, wild individual to one who was sitting in his right mind and possessed with the righteousness of God.

After this amazing encounter with Jesus, the man wanted to remain with him, and he requested this. However, Jesus told him to let everyone know what Jesus has done. In this particular story, Jesus was encouraging the man to reconnect with his family and friends within the vicinity. It was time for him to be in touch with those who loved him, to re-establish his links and ties to his wife and children, if he had any. He would have ample opportunities to witness to others about the saving grace of Jesus, who has power over everything—not just over the natural world, but over demonic forces too.

Whilst the inhabitants of Gadarenes were busy shooing Jesus away from their coast, people were gathering elsewhere to welcome and accept him. That day, the Gadarenes were left in utter darkness because the light of Jesus's presence was not desired by them. That day, the Gadarenes were left chocked in the wallow of spiritual uncleanness and the depravity of sin, chained to its demands of pride, wantonness, and greed. Like the herds of swine, they, too, were hurtling towards the pit of destruction.

They were unable to realize just how naked they were because they were clothed in filthy garments of sin, shame, and addiction. They had the opportunity to experience freedom from fear, death, satanic strongholds, oppressive sin, and darkness. But by rejecting Jesus, they embraced those things instead.

Can we afford to keep Jesus away from our lives, when he alone is the only one whereby we can survive day-to-day living? Surely not. God's intention was for Christ to save sinners and bring many to repentance. Nonetheless, there are countries held in a satanic sway around the world that are afraid of Jesus; this is not necessarily because of his power, but it seems as if his very holy presence unsettles them.

In John 14:23, he states that,

if a man loves me, we will come ... and make our abode with him. For everyone that does evil hates the light, neither comes to the light, lest his deeds be discovered for everyone who does evil ... this is the condemnation, that light is come into the world and men loved darkness rather than light. (John 3:19–20)

But if our gospel is hid, it's hidden from those who are lost. In whom the god of this world has blinded the minds of them who believe not, lest the light of the glorious gospel of Christ who is the image of God, should shine unto them. (2 Corinthians 4:3–4)

Behold, I stand at the door and knock; if any man hears my voice, and open the door, I will come in to him, and sup with him, and him with me. (Revelation 3:20).

This invitation is very personal and signifies intimacy: dwelling and communing in the presence of God himself through Jesus Christ.

Solomon's song, in chapter 5:2, echoes the same sentiment of invitation, acceptance, and intimacy. '... it is the voice of my beloved that knocks, saying, "Open to me, my sister, my love, my dove, my undefiled: for my head is filled with dew, and my locks with the drops of the night."'

Sadly, we don't know the end of their story, but it's even sadder to know that if people in the land of Gadarenes had needed healing, deliverance, liberty, and the like, then they denied themselves of those things as a result of fear, terror, and sin. Don't let it happen to you. Jesus's invitation is as valid and real today as it was way back then.

There are countries around the world held in a grip, bound in invisible strong chains, 'because the god of this world has blinded them' (2 Corinthians 4:4) with pleasures, personal pursuits, and self-ambitions so that their focus is on pleasing the self—the carnal man—which is enmity towards God.

Today our society is ravaged with fear and anxiety. Pharmacists are happy to dish out antidepressant pills in a bid to cure unhappiness, dissatisfaction, ailments, and stress. And because the adversary is on the rampage, like a proverbial lion seeking whomsoever he can, he spares no prisoners. The objection of his modus operandi is to lead people into a state of delusion, complacency, mediocracy, unbelief, and power in serving the self.

Truly, the scriptures testify that 'for all that is in the world is the pride of lust, pride of eyes, pride of life' (1 John 2:16). We must at all costs strive to show people Jesus radiating in our lives, through gracious living and works following. People will then be convinced that he is really alive, and like the man of Gadarenes, they will acknowledge that he came to set the captives free.

THE SECRETS OF THE DESERT

WHEN GOD PLACES AN assignment or plan on your life, he will call you by name and tell you certain aspects of it. It is then your opportunity to decide to say, 'Yes, Lord, Send me!', or to resist and remain in your comfort zone.

As for the children of Israel, he had promised their forefathers (Abraham, Isaac, and Jacob) that they would become strangers in a foreign land (Egypt), but he would afterwards bring them into a land of promise—Canaan.

To Abraham he said, 'Unto your descendants will I give this land ...' (Genesis 12:7, 13:15). To Isaac he said, 'Sojourn in this land, ... unto your seed I will give all these countries ...' (Genesis 26:4). To Jacob he said '... a company of nations ... and kings shall come out of thy loins, And the land which I gave Abraham and Isaac, to you I will give it, and to your descendants after you ...' (Genesis 35:10–12; 28:13).

God will call us out from something, someone, or somewhere in order to begin our journeys to greatness or destiny. He may call us from a vicinity, career, environment, or situation and take us under his wings. He will always assure us of his constant presence.

The wandering in the wilderness typifies the common pilgrim walk of the Christian in his relationship with the Lord, including all its distractions and tests. The best thing we can do is to learn from our mistakes, understand and heed the lessons carefully, embrace the experiences, and endeavour to have a good finish, moving successfully into the third zone of blessing and favour.

Remember how God travelled with his people. He did so as a pillar of cloud by day and a pillar of fire by night, right amongst them as bodyguard over their lives, 24–7. At certain points of our lives, he may send individuals on his behalf to strengthen, exhort, and correct us so we will make the necessary adjustments in our walks.

In verse 2 of Numbers 33, we are told that Moses wrote down all the parts of the journey so that the children of Israel would remember the experiences of each location. As we travel along our own wilderness experiences like Moses and David, it is a good idea to journal our thoughts and experiences at each stop, whether good or bad, as the information will provide you with inner fuel and help lift your faith as you contemplate the wonders of God's love in your life and the wisdom learnt from them.

Another idea you could use to make the journey memorable is to mark the occasion with an event that reminds you that something good is waiting for you on the other side. The Lord didn't reveal that the path to the children of Israel's first place of arrival would be through the wilderness. Surely that would have frightened them off! The Lord promised a land full of plenty that would be for them, their children, and their grandchildren to inherit—forever.

Listed below are all the stopping places from Succoth to Abel-shittim, where the children of Israel travelled through, the events that occurred there, and the actual meanings behind each location. The wilderness (or desert) of Sin is located between Elim and Mount Sinai The name is sometimes given as Zin; it is the same place.

Numbers 33:3 tells us that the Passover was held on the fourteenth day in the first month (Abib), which is associated with the month of April. Only those who were of Israelite lineage were able to participate in the solemn ceremony, including the servants that were purchased with money and were circumcised. Foreigners and hired help were not permitted. This event happened hurriedly, symbolizing Jesus's death on the cross. Every Israelite resident partook of this important festivity prior to leaving the land that had been their home for 430 years (Exodus 12:40–41).

They finally left behind Egypt, the land of servitude and bondage, on the fifteenth day of the first month, and from there moved unto Succoth.

Succoth

In Numbers 33:5, the word 'Succoth' means 'tents'. This was their first temporary stop. Nomads and Bedouin folk frequently moved around in deserts, always pitching their tents and then folding them up in search of a better location, especially for their livestock (pasture and water) and expansion (children and other people).

Like the nomads, the Israelites unrolled and pitched their tents at every location, stopping for varying lengths of time. The huge vastness of the desert was able to accommodate everybody. It took time to erect a tent and drive huge stakes into the ground to secure it against the external elements of the weather, but the tents were large and strong enough to contain the families, children, servants, and livestock.

Listed amongst seven celebrations in Leviticus 23 (verses 40–43) is the Feast of Tabernacles, which the Israelites were to participate in. They did this by cutting off the branches and leaves of good, strong trees—including palm trees and willows—and they rejoiced before the Lord God for seven days. It was a feast unto the Lord kept in the seventh month, Tishri (between the fifteenth and the twenty-first of September or October) throughout their generations. The Lord declared it as a statute (a lawful holiday), which was to be a perpetual reminder that the Lord allowed them to dwell in booths when he brought them out of the land of Egypt. They were also reminded to teach their children about the traditions and explain, when asked, why they did those things, so that the children in turn would pass it down unto the next generation.

The Feast of Tabernacles was also known by another name: Succoth or Sukkot. It is a Jewish holiday still observed today that originated during the autumn in the harvest time, when families spent time together in Canaan remembering the times when they moved along in tents. The shelters consisted of walls framed with wood and canvas, whilst the roofs were loosely covered with cut branches and leaves, leaving space for the stars to be seen at night. The tents were decorated with flowers, leaves, and fruit.

As we depart from the land of Sin—Egypt, or the comfort zone—we move into the next zone of preparation, sanctification, purging, and pressure.

The secret of Succoth tells us that the wilderness sojourn is not a permanent fixture but is one of continual movement. We dwell in our earthly homes for only a predetermined period of time that is unknown to us but is known to God. One day we will leave behind the homes we have lived in—regardless of location—for a certain amount of time. In the meantime, we must maintain them, pay for them, and keep them in good condition on this side of life. Furthermore, we must also keep our physical bodies in optimal condition, as they are home to the Holy Spirit who abides within.

As citizens of the kingdom of God, we must seek those things which are above and remember that in God's domain there are many mansions, and that Jesus has gone to prepare a place for us so that where he is, we will be there likewise. Until then we must journey on until the day that we exchange our earthly home for a heavenly one.

Etham

Numbers 33:6-7 tells us that Etham (meaning 'sea-bound') was at the edge of the wilderness. This suggests a point of no return. Otherwise, it would be like saying that one has regrets about leaving, and the only way back would be into sin (Egypt) and the only way ahead is forwards, towards destiny.

At some point, the Egyptians—who were burying their firstborn—soon realized and regretted releasing the Israelites, who left with the wealth of Egypt in tow. They wanted them back to complete their building projects. God revealed to Moses that he would harden Pharaoh's heart and that he would get honour from them; they would know that he is the Lord.

Pharaoh, along with his six hundred chariots, horses and captains, pursued the people. They had a lot of ground to cover, but God had a plan. 'Fear not, stand still, and see the salvation of the Lord, which he will show to you today: for the Egyptians whom you have seen today, you shall see them again no more forever. The Lord shall fight for you, and you shall hold your peace. (Exodus 14:13–14)

The children of Israel didn't require an aeroplane or need to create a last-minute boat to contain all the people. God instructed Moses to hold aloft his rod as he rolled back the waters of the mighty Red Sea, and they walked right through. How the story ends is just as fascinating as how the story began: their enemies were swallowed up in the midst of the waters. In the song of Moses, he proclaimed that Palestine, Edom, Moab, and the inhabitants all around had heard about it and were afraid! (see Exodus 15:15)

At the Red Sea, the people needed to walk through it so that the chains of bondage, Egyptian thinking, and stains of sin could be removed in the heart of the sea amidst the spray of waters. They were walking into a newness of life, away from the land associated with iniquity, sorcery, and spiritual death. Here their sins would be symbolically washed away, but the real work would begin on the testing grounds of the wilderness.

Similarly, the Red Sea for every believer in Christ is a threshold we all cross from 'death to spiritual life'. (See 1st Corinthians 10:2.) '… all were baptized under the cloud into the Sea …' This is spiritual death. 'If any man be in Christ he's a new creature.' (2 Corinthians 5:17). This means physical death for their enemies; they were drowned. Bury the old man and his deeds. (See Romans 6:3–12 and Colossians 2:12). And arise out of the water to newness of life, living unto sanctification and holiness. Certainly, these things happen when we leave our 'Egypt'— the world of sin—behind, confess or repent of our sins, and, as a result, get baptized. (See 1 Peter 3:21 and Ephesians 5:26–27).

The secret of Etham tells us that when we leave the life of sin behind us, we must be baptized to wash off its filth and the stench of our pasts in order to begin life anew in the land of purging and sanctification. Whilst it isn't an instantaneous transformation, it is an outward expression of informing the world that you are rejecting a sinful life in exchange for living a holy one.

Pi-Hahiroth

Numbers 33:7-8 brings us to Pi-Hahiroth (meaning 'the place of sedges' [sedges being flowers that typically grow in wet ground]). This was the start of a new beginning away from slavery, Egyptian worship, and philosophy. They were on the cusp of the old life and were edging forward towards a different way of living. They were at the entrance of rediscovery and learning about God being known as 'I AM THAT I AM' (Exodus 3:14) and what that life could potentially become.

The people were exchanging the life of brick-making labour, which involved adding straw to mud to strengthen the bricks, which were hardened in the heat of the Middle-Eastern sun. God was exchanging that harsh lifestyle for a land where their labours and toils would be much simpler and easier to accomplish.

The children of Israel were being uprooted from a life of sin and were being moved to be planted elsewhere. 'You brought a vine out of Egypt: you have cast out the heathen and planted it. You prepared room before it, and didst cause it to take deep root, and it filled the land' (Psalm 80:8–9). These verses are a reference to the children of Israel as being his special 'plant' whom he transferred and replanted from Egypt into Canaan, in keeping with his covenantal oath with the patriarchs.

The secret of Pi-Hahiroth tells us that Flowers can represent growth and new beginnings—a brand-new start filled with bright colours of hope and a future. Personal characteristics would be severely tried in the training ground of correction and sanctification. Flowers naturally grow under the normal environmental conditions of rain, heat, and storm. The Israelites were subject to the spiritual climes of God's chastening, with loving correction.

We must find our roots in Christ and become grounded in the knowledge that the Lord loves those whom he chastens and corrects.

We can adapt anywhere that God chooses to place us, because when he plants us, no one can uproot us. It doesn't matter what is thrown our way, because the Lord of heaven and earth will ensure that we are grounded in him and that we develop in all knowledge, maturity and righteousness in his name.

Migdol

Numbers 33:8 states that the people struck camp at Migdol (meaning 'tower') and departed to cross the Red Sea, the name of which was based not on its colour but on its reedy appearance. It was known as the Sea of Reeds. If we are to move into greatness, then we must all come to the Red Sea experience. Why? Because it is symbolic of a crucified life in Christ. (See 1 Corinthians 10:1–4).

At the tower, God would prove to be a lookout for his people. He would ensure that they were given more than abundant provisions for their daily needs, totally protected and watched over. At a watchtower, intelligence is gathered and communications are sent back and forth to inform the officer in command (in this case, Moses) about the best strategies against the foes. The enemies found God to be the undefeatable deity who opened the Red Sea and swallowed up the Egyptians with the same hand.

The secret of Migdol tells us that the name of the Lord is a strong tower where the righteous may run to and be safe. Being his son or daughter holds many privileges, one of them being all-round protection from seen and unseen dangers.

Marah

In Numbers 33:8-9, the name Marah means 'Bitter' (Exodus 15:22–23). Some general aspects of the wilderness terrain are sparse ground, dust, storm clouds, wild animals, barrenness, humidity, and lack of water resources. After three days in the desert, the children of Israel found no water, and when they did, it was too bitter to drink. The place where the children of Israel were gathered was called Marah.

But there was a solution: As Moses called upon the Lord, he showed him a tree which had made the waters sweet when he had cut it down and cast it into the waters. It was here that God made an ordinance and said,

If you will carefully listen to the voice of the Lord your God, and will do that which is right in his sight, and will give ear to his commandment, and keep all his statutes, I will put none of these diseases upon you, which I have brought upon the Egyptians: for I am the Lord that heals you. (Exodus 15:26)

One of the secrets of the desert is the realization of knowing that in our 'sanctification programme' designed by God, we must drink the 'bitter water'. Why? Because there are medicinal properties that aid the body through inner cleansing and detoxification. Jesus himself drank the contents of the bitter cup (Matthew 26:39).

Jesus's extreme pain and suffering meant that he was completely qualified to forgive everyone, despite their crimes, for their transgressions, because he was the spotless sacrificial lamb who became sin and who knew no sin.

The brothers James and John, who were also followers of Jesus, boldly claimed that they could drink from the same cup that Jesus drank from, in response to his question found in Matthew 20:22, 24. When bitter water is available, we should not refuse it. The bitter water can be disappointment, slander, rejection, scorn, humiliation, revilement, betrayal, and so forth. But know that the Lord is there and will keep you balanced as long as you stick with the programme. He will grant an extra measure of grace that will allow you to bear the circumstances you are faced with.

Whilst it is not pleasant to drink bitter water, it is both necessary and life-changing. We can call upon him and be assured of his assistance: 'This poor man cried, and the Lord heard him, and saved him out of all his troubles' Psalm 34:6.

As babies, we were inoculated in order to build up our immune systems and our resistance towards various diseases. We had portions of some viruses injected inside us so that we could withstand the maximum effects of the strains. The children of Israel received their water sweetened because they complained. The trees were cut down, which helped make the water easier to swallow.

In the same way as sucking a raw lemon causes us to pucker our mouths, God wants us to experience the 'nasty' experience of tribulation in order for us to grow, mature, gain wisdom and insight, and ultimately develop emotional stability under trying difficulties. This is crucial as the spiritual war against God's children (by faith in Jesus) intensifies. We must learn how to fight offensively in the spiritual realm as soldiers of the cross, not fearing for our lives.

That's why it is so important to drink of the bitter water and endure without complaining. Nothing in life, unfortunately, remains 'sweet' or straightforward all the time. Bad times happen. Sometimes when a problem strikes us from out of the blue, we need to know how to respond. God has placed emotional and psychological triggers in our bodies that enable us to tap into coping mechanisms so we can deal with issues that may appear traumatic, frightening, or painful.

The secret of Marah tells us that the bitter cup of testing has the potential to flush out our fleshly desires and toxins from within our lives and uncover any sinful motives, in order to bring us into true alignment of holiness and cleansing. He doesn't promise us that this water will taste good, but the internal workings from it will effect righteousness if we endure to the end.

Elim

Numbers 33:9-10 mentions Elim (meaning 'oaks' or 'trees'). As the children moved further on, they came to Elim, where significantly there were twelve fountains (or wells) of water and seventy palm trees.

Somebody counted them! That meant there was a well for each tribe and trees sufficient for their animals to graze from. They camped there for several days before moving on to their next stop.

Oak trees are reputable for being one of the most loved trees in the world. With very strong roots which grow downwards as well as upwards, they are symbolic of strength, fortitude, resistance, and knowledge. Spiritually speaking, they represent the righteousness of God. With a lifespan of between one hundred and three hundred years for most species reveals, they have a propensity for great longevity, considering they start off as acorns! It has been said that the strongest oak tree is the one that stands in the open, where it is compelled to struggle for its existence against the wind and rain and the scorching sun.

The secret of Elim tells us that, like the great oak tree, God is eternal, faithful, dependable, merciful, righteous, and strong. He never fails to deliver. The twelve wells of water prove that he leads us besides the still waters and refreshes our souls.

On the fifteenth day of the second month (Iyyar/Ziw), the congregation came to the wilderness of Sin situated between Elim and Sinai.

Dophkah

Numbers 33:12-13 mentions Dophkah (meaning 'drover' [one who drives cattle or sheep]). Like sheep, the people were herded into the wilderness on an adventure that would change their lives forever. This was not about merely walking for the sake of walking. This was about relying upon God, following instructions from Moses as their leader, and moving at His pace. With His presence leading the way, the travelling was made all the easier.

The Holy Spirit drove Jesus into the wilderness after his baptism in the River Jordan. He wasn't fully ready to pursue his God-ordained mission. There Jesus fasted and prayed for forty days and nights. Satan appeared on the scene and tempted him in three areas: the lust of the flesh (bread), the lust of eyes (materialism), and the pride of life (worship and self-gratification). The task ahead was demanding and required total reliance and focus upon his Father (God). Many of the giants of God were wilderness people: the patriarchs Abraham, Isaac, and Jacob; David; Daniel; Elijah; and Paul, to name but a few. The desert is a place where we can be alone with God, away from the day-to-day clutter and distractions.

As we learn from the Secret of Dophkah, we must get ready to be driven by the wind of the Holy Spirit. Whatever adversarial winds of conflict blow, know that God will buffet them and prepare you for any opposition that may come your way. You will be tempted in areas that will affect your eyes, your mind and perception, and your desire for power and glory. It is here that we are reminded that the Lord God is to be feared and worshipped only.

Alush

Numbers 33:13-14 mentions Alush (meaning 'crowd'). There was a crowd of over one million people who were gathered in the wilderness. However, God dealt with every one of them and catered to all of their individual needs. Our relationship with him poses no threat to the next person. Look at Moses; he went to the tent of meeting and maintained his fellowship with God.

The crowd was made up of twelve tribes. The Levite tribe was chosen to minister before the Lord on behalf of the congregation. A portion of the offering was allotted to them and their families for their service. Provisions were made for the high priest also. No one was missed.

The crowd was made up of men, women, boys, girls, pregnant mothers, and the mixed multitude: Egyptians who had converted to the religion of the Hebrews and were tagging along. This crowd was like sheep led throughout the desert by the faithful shepherd Moses. These people would journey into unknown territories needing to be fed, watered, rested, and taught how to fully depend upon the Lord.

They would receive instructions that would facilitate them for the rest of their lives.

The secret of Alush tells you that you must develop your own one-on-one time with God. He's waiting to provide you with his companionship and spend quality time with you. In a crowded area, every face has a name and a story behind it. Every single person is unique and special to Him. In his presence, there is fullness of joy.

Rephidim

Numbers 33:14-15 mentions Rephidim (meaning 'rest'). God commanded a rest day for his people by introducing the Sabbath day on the seventh day of the week—a day which he also chose to rest on as an example to mankind. Psalm 23 shows us that David knew the importance of rest, peace, and meditation when he says of God, 'He makes me to lie down in green pastures and leads me by still waters and restores my soul.' Numbers 9:15–23 informs us of the people pitching their tents whenever the cloud rested.

Along the way, there were times when the people stayed at a particular location for a time ranging from two days to a month or even a year. During those times, babies were born, people died and were buried, and marriages were formed.

At Rephidim, the Amalekite nation came out against Israel and fought against them. On that day, Moses stood on the top of the hill with the rod of God in his hand, and whilst his hands were held high, Israel prevailed; but when his hands grew tired and dropped to his sides, the Amalekites began winning. To solve this dilemma, Moses utilized the strategy of unison and went up again with Aaron and Hur, who together held up his hands up until sunset (Exodus 17:10–1). The young Joshua defeated this hostile nation with the edge of the sword, and God commanded Moses to write down what he would do in the future, saying they had 'touched [his] people.' He went on: 'I will utterly put out the remembrance of (the tribe of) Amalek from under heaven.' (Exodus 17:14)

It was here that God said of those who would obey his voice and keep his covenant, 'you shall be a peculiar treasure unto me above all people; for all the earth is mine: and you shall be to me a kingdom of priests, and an holy nation'(Exodus 19:6).

The secret of the Rephidim tells us that God will not deprive his beloved children of rest (whether it be physical, emotional, psychological, or spiritual). When you rest in God, you can be assured of complete and total holistic restoration of the mind, body, and spirit, which you can enjoy. You can relax in his love and in his presence. 'There remains a rest for the people of God. So let us labour to enter into that rest, else any man falls after the same example of unbelief' (Hebrews 4:9, 11).

Sinai

Numbers 33:15-16 mention Sinai (meaning 'bushy'). It was at this location that the laws were handed down to the newly formed nation Israel. Moses had already experienced the Lord's presence some forty years earlier in the phenomenal appearance of the burning bush that was not consumed. The Lord revealed himself to Moses as the God of Abraham, the God of Isaac, and the God of Jacob (Exodus 3:6).

'Out of Egypt I have called my son' (Hosea 11:1; Matthew 2:15). This was the opportunity for the children of Israel to learn about God, have a relationship with him, and come to know his holiness, his mind, and his heart. They were a nation who were to be a peculiar people and a royal priesthood to the rest of the world.

Moses ascended the mountain and stayed for forty days and nights to receive the Ten commandments, which were written on two tablets of stone, including instructions about the construction of the tabernacle system, the furniture and clothes for the high priest and ministering Levites, and laws regarding health, marriage, the judicial system, burnt offerings, food consumption, respect and dignity of people, money, sex, hygiene, children, interrelationships, various prohibitions, matters regarding military service, the home, the welfare of animals, the orphaned, the widowed, strangers, slaves, tithing, holy days, festivities, worship, daily living, and many more things.

At Mount Sinai, God called the congregation to consecration and made his presence seen and felt with terrifying thunder and lightning, with the voice of a trumpet sounding extremely loudly. Also, whilst the mount was covered in smoke, the Lord descended on it in fire; it was like the smoke of a furnace. The people were strongly cautioned not to approach the mountain to try to gaze up at God. They were not even to touch it; otherwise, they would be instantly slain. That included the animals too. The only person permitted to get close to the quaking mountain was Moses.

Whilst Moses was away, the people became restless and bored. So in his absence they inveigled poor Aaron, his brother, to make a golden calf that they could worship. They had already broken two of the laws from the Ten Commandments before they had even received them; namely, 'You shall have no other gods ...' and 'You shall not make any graven image ...' (Exodus 20:3-4).

The commandments, ordinances, statutes, and laws were given to teach the children of Israel the knowledge of the Lord and to make them instrumental in showing the way to the other nations around. They were to be a beacon to the masses—a lighthouse to those who needed salvation and instruction—because the oracles of God were committed to them (Romans 3:2).

The greatest aspect of the commandments was called, 'The Shammah': 'Hear O Israel, The Lord our God is one Lord: And you shall love the Lord your God with all your heart, and with all your soul, and with all your might' (Deuteronomy 6:4–5). This was followed with,

And you shall love your neighbour as yourself. (Leviticus 19:18)

Oh that there were such an heart in them, that they would fear me, and keep all my commandments always, that it might be well with them, and with their children forever! (Deuteronomy 5:29)

Throughout the Torah are words similar to the effect of 'I am the Lord' (Leviticus 19:18), 'You shall know that I am the Lord,' and 'I am the Lord your God' (Leviticus 18:13). This interestingly crops up repeatedly as an undercurrent theme throughout the prophetic book of Ezekiel. This informs us that God's unconditional and intentional relationship towards Israel was exceedingly intertwined with the covenantal oath which he established through Abraham, Isaac, and Jacob.

The Lord God also mentioned the reason for giving the Israelites the land:

For all these abominations the men of the land have done, which were before you, and the land is defiled;) That the land doesn't spew you out, when you defile it, as it spewed out the nations that were before you. Defile not yourselves in any of these things: [listed in the book of Leviticus, in particular]: for in all these the nations are defiled which I cast out before you. (Leviticus 18:24,27–28)

Something else marvellous happened to Moses.

And it came to pass, when Moses came down from Mount Sinai with the two tables of stone his face shone, (but he did not know this). And when Aaron and all the children of Israel saw Moses, the skin of his face shone; and they were afraid to come near to him ... And till Moses had done speaking with them, he put a veil on his face. But when Moses went in before the Lord to speak with him, he took the veil off, until he came out ... And the children of Israel saw the face of Moses, that the skin of Moses' face shone: and Moses put the veil upon his face again, until he went in to speak with God. (Exodus 34:29–35)

It was also here that the first census took place. It happened on the first day of the second month, in the second year after the tribes departed from Egypt, in the tabernacle of the congregation. Moses presided over the mammoth task and, at the Lord's command, selected twelve respectable princes of the tribes of their fathers who numbered the congregation from twenty years old and upwards. The individual tribes were registered and showed their pedigrees, which took some time to complete. The total amount numbered in the first census was six hundred thousand three hundred and fifty three, excluding the tribe of Levi and those yet to be born.

(Side note: Just as clarification, because of their disobedience to take the land when instructed, they died in the wilderness instead. Those who came out of Egypt aged twenty had a maximum life expectancy of just sixty years, provided they survived the entire forty years in the desert. At the age of thirty, the life expectancy maximum was seventy years. Squeezed within that concept were the multiple deaths and the multiple births that occurred throughout the sojourn.)

Psalm 90 is a prayer centred around Deuteronomy 32. Moses, the man of God, gives them a reminder in verses 9 and 10:

For all our days are passed away in the wrath: we spend our years as a tale that is told. The days of our years are threescore years and ten; and if by reason of strength they be fourscore years, yet is their strength labour and sorrow; for it is soon cut off, and we fly away.

The secret of Sinai is that it's the place where God instructs us on the principles of living righteously. This is directly connected to how we conduct our personal lives, our conduct with God, and our conduct with others. It's up to us whether we choose to abide by them and enjoy a successfully blessed life or abandon them to our own neglect and folly. 'Choose today whom you will serve' (Joshua 24.15). 'Choose life so that you and your descendants may live' (Deuteronomy 30:19d).

Kibroth-Hattaavah

Numbers 33:16-17 mentions Kibroth-Hattaavah (meaning 'the graves of lusts'). This is another location worth mentioning. It was here that the people craved meat because they were bored with manna—the bread of heaven. As a result of their complaining, God gave them their desire to the extent that they were killed by the plague, through their noses.

In Numbers chapter 11:1-21, the children again complain to Moses and the seventy elders who had received the prophetic anointing. God sent word that he would send a strong wind, and quails from the sea covered the ground two cubits high (approximately three feet) all around the encampment.

On our spiritual journeys, there's got to be a place where we can dump our fleshly cravings and motives in the grave, never to rise again. In the land of purging our natural tendencies for the self-gratification of pride, ambition, wealth, fame, or acclaim, these need to be placed into the ground and replaced by more of God's words. In Deuteronomy 8:3, we are reminded that 'Man doesn't, live on merely bread alone, but by every word that comes out of the mouth of God.'

Being fed with the heavenly bread was an extremely important lesson for the Israelites to learn—a test designed to discover just how willing they were to endure a 'normal' situation.

Some circumstances do not always appear pleasant; they can be painful, tedious, or monotonous. But are we, as Christian pilgrims, willing to put up with it on a temporary basis or for as long as it takes before the breakthrough comes? God has already assured us that we'll get into the Promised Land. In the meantime, we must be prepared to put up with those things which may irritate us, bore us, frustrate us, or even try our patience, by meditating on the positive words and promises close to our hearts.

Numbers chapter 11:24-29 highlights the necessity for patience and contentment as we travel on with the Lord. An example of enjoying God's word is hidden amongst verses 24–29, where Moses and the seventy elders are caught up in the spiritual realm, prophesying incessantly, as the Holy Spirit is distributed from Moses by God.

It was like experiencing a mini-Pentecost, as mentioned in Acts 2. Two outsiders got caught up in the moment, as noted by Joshua, to which Moses replied, 'Would God that all the Lord's people were prophets, and that the Lord would put his spirit in them.' The names of these individuals were Eldad (meaning 'loved of God') and Medad (meaning 'love'). You see, when this happens, nothing else truly matters other than that you are in the presence of the Lord, feasting on heavenly manna.

When we decide to permit our fleshly desires to dictate our whims and we grant them priority over God's will, we forfeit the possible blessings that are attached to his commands; he always has way better things in store for us. 'Oh taste and see that the Lord is good!' (Psalm 34:8). Having food and raiment, let's be content (1 Timothy 6:8).

The secret of Kibroth-Hattaavah tells us that we are to let the flesh be dumb and submissive to our spirits. Don't allow yourself to be corrupted by the influences and indulgences of the world; otherwise, they will sink you into hell. For all that is in the world, the lust of the flesh, the lust of the eyes, and the pride of life are not of the Father but are of the world (1 John 2:16).

Hazeroth

Numbers 33:17-18 mentions a location called Hazeroth (meaning 'villages'). 'Village' is defined in the *Collins Dictionary* as 'a small group of houses in a country area.' Interestingly enough, the children of Israel were a group of people set within twelve tribes plus the mixed multitude of Egyptians who tagged along, perhaps as a result of their having viewed the manifestation of God's power that was displayed in Egypt.

The twelve tribes walked in formation—in the shape of the cross, as per God's instructions—through the desert after the census. The arrangement was spectacular, with the tabernacle placed centrally amongst them, symbolizing God's presence, including all the holy objects and furniture transported by members of the families of Levi.

The Kohathites were responsible for the heavy furniture, such as the table, ark, candlestick, altars, and the vessels of the sanctuary. The Gershonites were responsible for the tent, the coverings, the hangings of the court, the curtains, and the cords. The Merarites were in charge of the small things, such as the boards of the tabernacle, the bars, the pillars, the sockets, the vessels, and the pins and their cords. The souls that exited Egypt were six hundred thousand men on foot, excluding women and children.

It was also at this very location that Miriam complained to her brother Aaron about his choice of wife and God's preference of Moses. As a result of her gripe, he struck her with leprosy. Meek brother Moses interceded for her, but God denied his request. She had to remain in her leprous condition for an entire week before the people could move on to their next location.

These villagers, though wanderers in a desert land, were divinely positioned and destined for blessing in the form of an everlasting territory that was already promised to their forefathers.

The secret of Hazeroth tells us that as a global family of God, no matter where we are located in the world, our nationalities, races, colours, and creeds are inexplicably linked together by the bloodline of Jesus Christ. As people of God, we are a chosen generation, a royal priesthood, a holy nation, and a peculiar people (Deuteronomy 7:6). At Jesus's return, regardless of nationality, language, or class, his chosen people will stand before him as his perfect bride, arrayed in white linen. What a glorious prospect!

Rithmah

Numbers 33:18-19 mentions Rithmah (meaning 'bushy'). Even when situations or circumstances seem insignificant or just routinely ordinary, we must still persevere. We are not told how long the Israelites camped there, but things were always happening on a regular basis in their ordinary lives. It is worth consideration that babies were continually being born and reared, people were getting married, and people died and were buried.

It could be that in that area the Israelites were surrounded by bushes. Bushes are important for climate control, stabilization of soil, ecosystem water balance, and the nutrition and safety of livestock, birds, fungi, and other such creatures. Their appearance in the wilderness was required and needful.

In our own waiting, we must learn how to possess our souls. Be earnest in your quest to be a better steward of the kingdom of heaven. Every day presents an opportunity to improve yourself in the land of testing and sanctification. When everywhere around you just looks like bushes and no substance, remember that God's promises regarding your life and destiny remain unchanged.

The secret of Rithmah tells us that we are not to despise small beginnings. Even in the ordinary and the mundane, God is testing our hearts to see whether we will still trust him.

Rimmon-Parez

Numbers 33:19-20 mention Rimmon-Parez (meaning 'pomegranates of the wrath'). This name comprises two words, 'Rimmon' and 'Pérez' (meaning 'pomegranates' and 'wrath') This could be considered as a reference to the unfruitful works of unrighteousness.

During the journey, the Israelites wanted some idea of what Canaan looked like. So after soliciting Moses in chapter 13 of Numbers, and at God's command, he selected twelve men, one from each tribe, to go and search the land for forty days. In their reports, they were to include the following details:

- the type of people who lived there—strong, weak, few, or many
- whether the land itself was good or bad, fat or lean
- the conditions of the cities: whether the people lived in tents or strongholds
- whether there was wood or not
- evidence of fruit, which was to be brought back (It was the season for ripe early grapes.)

The names of the people sent to spy out the land are also significant. Let's take a look at their meanings.

Tribe	Name of Spy	Meaning
Reuben	Shammua	Heard
Simeon	Shaphat	Judge
Judah	Caleb*	Able
Issachar	Igal	Redeemed
Ephraim	Oshea (Joshua)*	Saviour
Benjamin	Palti	Deliverance
Zebulon	Gaddiel	Fortune Of God
Manasseh	Gaddi	Fortunate
Dan	Ammiel	People Of God
Asher	Sethur	Hidden
Naphtali	Nahbi	Secret
Gad	Geuel	Majesty Of God

- The men shown with an asterisk (*) were the ones who entered Canaan.

Twelve men with mighty titles started off their expedition with great promise. They travelled and searched extensively from the wilderness of Zin unto Rehob, right through to Hebron, where the children of Anak dwelt. They cut down a cluster of grapes which they bore upon their shoulders on a pole, along with some pomegranates and figs. On their return into the wilderness of Paran near Rimmon-Parez, they showed to the congregation the delicious fruits of the land, and they thoroughly agreed that it indeed flowed with 'milk and honey'.

Ten of those men decidedly spoke negatively about the residents who lived there. They focused on the fact that the Amalekites, the Jebusites, and the Amorites dwelt in the mountains and that the Canaanites and the giants lived there. Added to that aspect was that they saw themselves as 'ants' in comparison.

Their report could have read something like this: 'We have heard from the Judge of heaven and earth that we are well able to obtain our promised legacy as his redeemed people. Our Saviour will grant us the deliverance needed to overcome and conquer all the giants who are bigger than us. And we can crush them, because our God is with us. The fortune of God has made us fortunate. He has hidden our land from everyone else to prevent them from obtaining it. What was once a secret is now made known to us. All praise to the majesty of God.'

Instead, ten of their evil reports were partially tainted. They mentioned the fruits and that the land was good. However, their words were negatively peppered with phrases like the following: 'the giants', '... We are like ants, in their sight ...', 'We cant' ...', and 'We are not able ...' This shattered the hopes and expectations of the people who listened carefully to their words.

Caleb and Joshua pressed hard to convince the people listening that they were able to possess the land. However, the other men poured cold water over their statements because of what they had seen with their eyes; they just didn't believe it was possible for them to defeat the stronger nations. The people listening were so angry with the two honest men that they took up stones to kill them!

After hearing the reports, the Israelites wept in their tents that night and murmured, saying that it would have been better had they died in Egypt or in the wilderness. That was fulfilled because of their unbelief, and the ten wicked men who were granted the opportunity to see a glimpse of the wonderful land died also.

God was faithful to them as promised and allowed the orphaned generation to enjoy the privileges of Canaan without their parents. Those who left Egypt were the seeds, or pomegranates, of God's wrath.

The seeds of doubt, disbelief, murmuring, rebellion, fear, and disobedience were sown long before they entered the wilderness, and they died that way because of the unbelievers' constant provocations and unfaithfulness.

Later on, their children fell into the same rut, just as God had disclosed to Moses in Deuteronomy 31:16, and as a result they suffered the same fate at the hands of their hostile enemies. It seemed they didn't learn the same lessons their parents had failed to grasp.

The secret of Rimmon-Parez tells us to be fruitful in the things that really matter and that ultimately bring glory to God. We must believe that God is able to fulfil what he has promised in our lives. Our godly works (or achievements) must be coupled with faith. In James 2:20, we are challenged with the phrase 'faith without works is dead' and the notion that works without faith are also useless.

The ten men had the physical fruit, produce, but they failed to believe or have their own conviction that God would give them the land, though they saw it with their own eyes.

Libnah

Numbers 33:20-21 mention Libnah (meaning 'white'). When the tabernacle system was finished, it was erected and made ready for the Levitical priesthood to implement the services as God's ministers. Their garments, which they wore when they performed their duties before the Lord, were made from fine white linen.

The children of Israel sinned constantly but were given countless opportunities during their sojourn to repent and live holy again. The whole idea of the tabernacle and sacrificial system was designed from God's viewpoint that since Adam's sin, man would always need forgiveness and cleansing through the shedding of blood. Whenever the blood of the bullock, goat, sheep, or turtledove was spilt, then it was the duty of the Levitical priesthood to offer it up before God so that the person could receive atonement. This system was to be used until the perfect 'sacrifice' was revealed to the world much later on in the form of his son, Jesus Christ, the holy Lamb of God.

God was often angry with the dissatisfied crowd. However, his greatest disappointment with them was their lack of faith and unbelief that he could keep his word and bring them into Canaan. Many of their statements ran like this: '… did you bring us out here to die?' ' … Why did you bring us out of Egypt? …'

Today, if you will hear his voice, harden not your heart, as in the provocation, and as in the day of temptation in the wilderness: When your fathers tempted me, proved me, and saw my work. Forty years long was I grieved with this generation, and said, 'It is a people that do err in their heart, and they have not known my ways:' Unto whom I swore in my wrath that they should not enter into my rest. (Psalm 95:7–11)

These verses refer to the time when the Israelites had crossed the Red Sea and had entered the wilderness section of Rephidim—rest. Several days in, they were thirsty and questioned God by saying, 'Give us something to drink ... Is the Lord among us, or not? ...' (Exodus 17:2a, 7b).

The prophet Isaiah, in Exodus 1:18–19, admonishes God's people by saying, 'Come now, and let us reason together ... though your sins be as scarlet, they shall be as white as snow; though they be red like crimson, they shall be as wool.'

Additional reminders were inserted within the message as he spoke. These were reminders they were fully acquainted with, because it was written in the Torah of how they were to behave and conduct themselves. 'Learn to do well; seek judgment, relieve the oppressed, judge the fatherless, plead for the widow. Wash yourselves, (spiritually) and be clean, put away the evil of your doings from before mine eyes; cease to do evil' (Isaiah 1:16–17).

The secret of Libnah tells us that if we will allow the tests of the wilderness to change us positively, God will ensure that we come out of it as 'white'—sanctified and suitable for his service (2 Timothy 2:20). As we sojourn the 'desert' of our lives, God's intention is, for us, holy, because He is holy. In Malachi 3:2, God declares himself as a Refiner's Fire and the Fuller's Soap. Historically, a fuller's soap was made up of chemicals and urine which bore a distinctively unpleasant odour but cleansed things very well.

Rissau

Numbers 33:21-22 mentions Rissau (meaning 'Ruins'). The experiences in the desert should have taught the people to trust in God and to remember that he only had the best in mind for them.

God wasn't prepared to give his precious children the land of blessing on a silver platter after their initial disobedience to take the land.

In the matter of Korah and the rebellion, fourteen thousand seven hundred people were struck with a plague sent from God and were destroyed because they murmured within themselves that Moses and Aaron had killed the people of the Lord. They ruined the opportunity to get into the land because of rebellion and provocation.

God settled this situation once and for all by telling Moses to ask each tribe to hand him a stick with the name of the tribe written upon it. Once he had done that, he was to lay all the sticks in the tabernacle overnight. The next morning, the rods were inspected, and amongst them was a rod that, without water or soil, had miraculously budded, bloomed, and blossomed; it belonged to the house of Levi.

That rod was laid up in the ark of the covenant, as a sign, alongside the copy of the Ten Commandments and the pot of manna.

In the wilderness, all our fleshly attributes and attitudes should look like ruins, destroyed and irreparable.

The Secret of Rissau tells us that we must let go of the things that would beset us and hinder us from entering our promised land.

Kehelathah

Numbers 33:23 mentions Kehelathah (meaning 'assembly'). Sadly, there were instances where the unity of the people here got them into a whole heap of trouble. Take, for instance, when Korah stirred up Dathan and Abiram against Moses's leadership. Consequently, that uprising led to those men, plus two hundred and fifty princes, being supernaturally swallowed up in the ground.

On their march through the wilderness, they went by the standard of the camp, according to Numbers 10. The first standard was led by Judah, who was represented by the face of a lion on the eastern side. The other tribes which made up that set were Issachar and Zebulon.

On the south side was the next standard, represented by the

face of a man. The other tribes which made up the set were Simeon and Gad.

On the west side, the standard was the face of an ox, led by the tribe of Ephraim. The tribes following this standard were Manasseh and Benjamin.

The last standard was led by the tribe of Dan and bore the face of an eagle. The other tribes which made up this set were Asher and Naphtali, with their captains.

It was a beautiful yet formidable sight to behold. It wasn't a rabble of people looking disorganized and walking with uncertainty. There was purpose in their walk as they marched in harmony towards their destiny. The tabernacle was centrally placed, symbolizing God's immediate presence in the midst of them.

God commanded Moses to inform Aaron to bless the children of Israel daily with a benediction, saying, 'The Lord bless you, and keep you: The Lord make his face shine upon you, and be gracious unto you. The Lord lift up his countenance upon you, and give you peace. (And they shall put my name upon the children of Israel; and I will bless them)' Numbers 6:23–27.

The secret of Kehelathah tells us that it is good when people dwell together in unity. Just ensure that you know and recognize who it is you are joining or assembling with. The power of unity, when harnessed righteously, produces phenomenal results. On the day of Pentecost, three thousand souls were added to the church in a single day by the preaching of Peter.

Shapher

Numbers 33:24 mentions Shapher (meaning 'bright'). This location happened to be near a mountain. Being near a mountain may not conjure thoughts of loveliness or brightness. It may look more like a blockage, distraction, blind spot, or boulder. Nevertheless, mountains may surround or be in the pathway of greatness, as one was for the children of Israel. But they kept moving. They weren't going to be stationed there forever; it was just part of the journey.

Some mountains don't need to be climbed over, but just walked around; but one must be mindful of the stones, wild snakes, and wild plants that may lie in one's path.

God's presence in the pillar of cloud and fire was a constant sight of brightness whether during day or night; this is proof that he was always with them, amongst them, and behind them throughout their wanderings.

Another feature of brightness is reflected in the breastplate of judgement, detailed in Exodus 28. It was crafted similarly to the ephod, with the colours of gold, blue, purple, and scarlet, and made of fine twined linen. It was square, and within that square were twelve stones set in rows of four, which represented the twelve tribes. The high priest wore the beautiful robe before the Lord and had the stones not only on his heart but also on his shoulders.

The first row was a sardius (ruby), topaz, carbuncle

The second row was an emerald, a sapphire, a diamond

The third row was a ligure, an agate, and an amethyst

The fourth row was a beryl, an onyx, a jasper

And the stones shall be with the names of the children of Israel, twelve, according to their names, like the engravings of a signet; every one with his name shall they be according to the twelve tribes. (Exodus 28:21,22)

And you shall take two onyx stones, and engrave on them the names of the children of Israel: Six of their names on one stone, and the other six names of the rest on the other stone, according to their birth ... And you shall put the two stones upon the shoulders of the ephod for stones of memorial unto the children of Israel: and Aaron shall bear their names before the Lord ... (Exodus 28:9)

The secret of Shapher tells us that physical mountains are not really hindrances, whilst spiritual ones are. We know we can conquer them in the name of Jesus Christ. 'Not by might, nor by power, but by my Spirit', says the Lord of Hosts. Our pathway is made brighter and lovelier in the knowledge that we're leaving from one place in order to reach another.

Haradah

Numbers 33:24-25 references Haradah (meaning 'quaking' or 'terror and fears'). There were real fears to be had in the harsh wilderness environment. But God had proven himself powerful and capable enough to deal with every single circumstance: hunger, thirst, being destroyed by wild animals, finding somewhere to lay their heads, protection from their enemies, clothing themselves, and babies being delivered without defects or difficulties. (None of the babies were born with any abnormalities or died, and none of the mothers miscarried). God had it all figured out.

In Psalms 23, we are reminded that when we walk through the valley of 'the shadow of death' we need not fear any evil, whether it looks like troubles, afflictions, assaults, or woes, which will inevitably come. Why? Because the Lord is with us; his rod of correction and loving chastening disciplines, and his staff of guidance, instruction, and encouragement will comfort us.

To expand on the 'shadow of death' included in this is the narrow path—the road less travelled—to walk: which is not for the faint-hearted. On it lie dangers, darkness, loneliness, traps and snares, and pits—deep holes to suck you in. 'Blessed is the man whose hope [confidence] is in the Lord' (Jeremiah 17:7).

He rained down manna from heaven daily, provided water from a rock on two occasions, and granted them favour from their Egyptian neighbours to retrieve the wealth that they were so deprived of whilst in slavery. Supernaturally, the soles of their shoes did not wear away; neither did their clothes rot or wear out in the trying terrain.

There were times when even Moses's leadership was challenged, with people wanting to stone him when things didn't go their way. In one instance, the people elected a captain to take them to Canaan;

they back-pedalled on their ideas after Joshua and Caleb encouraged them about the land.

The Secret of Haradah tells us that we have absolutely nothing to worry about, because we know without a shadow of a doubt that Jesus will sustain and keep us wherever we are. He who provides for the sparrows has an eye on our souls. 'Sanctify the Lord in your hearts/minds; let Him be your fear and your dread' (Isaiah 8:13).

Makheloth

Numbers 33:25-26 mentions Makheloth (meaning 'the meeting place').

And it came to pass when Moses went out unto the tabernacle, that all the people rose up, and stood every man at his tent door, and looked after Moses, until he was gone into the tabernacle. And it came to pass, as Moses entered into the tabernacle, the cloudy pillar descended and stood at the door of the tabernacle, and the Lord talked with Moses. And all the people saw the cloudy pillar stand at the tabernacle door: and all the people rose up and worshipped, every man in his tent door. And the Lord spoke to Moses face to face, as a man speaks unto his friend. And he turned again into the camp. Exodus 33:9–11.

Here was a man who had a very personal and intimate relationship with God, and everybody knew about it. It was evident in the showing of the cloudy pillar that stood at the door of the tabernacle. We are further told that God spoke with Moses face to face, as a man does with his friend. And as much as we know what 'the Lord said unto Moses' to tell the people, we are not informed about their most personal conversations. This tells us that even on our pilgrimage to the land of promise, literal or spiritually speaking, we can communicate with the Holy Spirit: tell him all about our troubles and struggles, sing, talk, or rationalize, if you will.

Later on in the book of Exodus, Moses asks to see God's glory as a sign of God's presence with him. The Lord replies that he has found favour in his sight and in response to his request tells him to hide in the cleft of the rock, adding that as he covers him with his hand, Moses will be able to see his back parts, but his face will not be seen.

The fire of his presence will cover us as a blanket of protection, mercy, and divine love. No other force, disaster, or distraction can interfere here. It is here where God gets up close and personal with us, and calls us to a higher level of intimacy. In Exodus 24, the nobles of the children of Israel experienced a unique insight of God's glory, which resembled the transfiguration of Christ. Even in this instance, God did not slay them but allowed them to gaze at the paved work of sapphire stone and the body of heaven in its transparency.

Throughout our trials, God wants us to meet with Him alone so we can experience divine intimacy, which Moses obviously enjoyed. Your 'tabernacle' could be your bedroom, your study room, or somewhere that's sacred between you and your Lover—a favourite spot. God wants us to reach a place of holiness so that his presence will not consume but rather will purify and intensify our desire for Him and His will alone.

It is through the communication of prayer that we develop a strong connection with the Father, who delights in sharing his heart with us. As we speak with him, he will teach us how to unlock the doors of heaven in order to get the answers and desires of our lives fulfilled. He says, 'No good thing will he withhold from them that walk uprightly' (Psalm 84:11). He will teach us the prayer language that goes up as a fireball into the courts of heaven; prayers that gives us unlimited access to the vaults of his kingdom: various examples of which can be found in the Bible.

Fellowship is what he craves from his children. As much as there were so many people in that wilderness, God had time for every single body. No one ever really has to be envious about God spending more time with one person or the other, because he loves us all.

The secret of Makheloth is that in the meeting place, we can encounter face-to-face experiences with God that we'll never forget. He shares revelations about himself and about us. Time spent with

Him is a worthwhile and valuable investment in the land of purging and sanctification. Meeting with God is a must in order to realign our values, strengths, and purposes for living.

Tahath

Numbers 33:26-27 mentions Tahath (meaning 'beneath', 'support', or 'fear of going down'). God had a particular interest in this people, as they were linked to his friend Abraham, the 'Father of many Nations' (Genesis 17:5). When Jacob and his family left Canaan to be fed during the famine by the generosity of Pharaoh in the land of Egypt, they were just a handful of people—seventy souls, to be precise. The Lord had promised to multiply them like the stars of heaven and the dust of the earth. That promise came true. Those who heard about this God and his exploits in Egypt heard about a nation deemed as powerful and special.

Moses reminded the people of how God had borne them up on eagles' wings and brought them unto himself. God supported them all the way through their ups and downs, including every smooth and dangerous track. He was right there, carrying and lifting them, because they were redeemed and precious 'as the apple of his eye' Deuteronomy 32:10).

Deuteronomy chapter 28 lists the blessings for obedience and the curses for disobedience. God was very serious about his relationship with his people Israel, even though they were not. Every effort was made to bless and support them so that they would become the envy of nations.

If they obeyed the Lord, they would be blessed in the city and the field with their children, food, cattle, and produce; their enemies would flee; and they would have the best of heaven. And what would be the result of this? 'All the people of the earth shall see that you are called by the name of the Lord; and they shall be afraid of you' (Deuteronomy 28:10).

The Secret of Tahath tells us that We are the head, and not the tail. We are above and not beneath as long as we listen and obey the commands of the Lord (Deuteronomy 28:13).

Even when it looks like we're 'going under', or sinking beneath the pressure of our tests and trials, the Lord will take us up. He will be the wind beneath our wings. We are never truly forsaken, because he has our backs.

Mithcah

Numbers 33:28-29 mentions Mithcah (meaning 'sweetness'). In the wilderness, the miraculous signs that were manifested by God were just a taste of good things to come—if they endured. Amidst the combination of the sour experiences alongside the sweet experiences were things that couldn't be avoided. The water at Marah that was bitter was made sweet. The manna was sweet. The destruction of their enemies without them having to lift a finger was sweet.

It was their unbelief, complaining, and constant provocations against God's provisions that soured the Israeli ex-slaves from ever getting into the Promised Land, which flowed with milk and honey. What was theirs was consequently given as a legacy to the next generation and grandchildren instead.

The secret of Mithcah tells us that God will replace our bitter experiences with the sweetest blessings that will flow abundantly in our souls. Job had it all, and he lost it all; but in his season of testing, he remained firm in his relationship with God. As a result, he was blessed with sweet success.

In order to truly appreciate sweetness, we must encounter experiences that feel like hell on earth; but in exchange, God will give us a foretaste of glory that leads to eternal life.

Hasmonah

Numbers 33:29-30 mentions Hasmonah (meaning 'fatness'). 'But Jeshurun grew fat, and kicked: you are grown fat, you are grown thick; you are covered with fatness; then he forsook God which made him, and lightly esteemed the Rock of his salvation' (Deuteronomy 32:15). This verse speaks symbolically of Israel. The name 'Jeshurun' means 'blessed'. Indeed they were a blessed nation through their spiritual heritage with Abraham, Isaac, and Jacob.

God fulfilled his word. They prospered, and everything that God had promised to them came true. They possessed the land of brooks, fig trees, vines, olive, honey, wheat and barley, maize, wine, and oil, but they soon forgot who their Maker was.

Wading throughout the scriptures from the book of Judges onwards, we soon discover a lengthy trail of stories filled with spiritual debauchery, idolatry, disobedience, and lawlessness. Unfortunately, this led to all kinds of punishments and captivity. Many of the prophets and judges were sent to warn the children of Israel of their unrelenting, backslidden ways. Just under half of the OT books alone relate to prophets whom God used to send messages to his wayward people.

The secret of Hasmonah tells us that the blessings of the Lord make us rich, and he adds no sorrow to this. We must ensure to always remember his goodness and praise his name continually; otherwise, the consequences for sin and forgetfulness are severe.

Moseroth

Numbers 33:30-31 mentions Moseroth (meaning 'bonds and chains'). This settlement would remind the Israelites who left Egypt about the harsh realities of slavery: being at the beck and call of their masters, the brutal beatings, and the hard slogging and labouring—especially with regard to making bricks for the construction of the treasure houses for the pharaohs.

They were free, but yet they still held a slave-like mentality. God was not just building a relationship with them but was building a special nation that would make the other nations around them sit up and pay attention.

Embedded within the code of ordinances is a chapter or two dedicated to explaining the usage of bondservants. These were slaves who were bound to service without wages. The Israelites were not allowed to use their own people who had fallen upon hard times, or impose usury for them to pay money back with increase. The proviso in that case was that 'he could be as a hired servant who could serve until the year of jubilee' (Leviticus 25:40). Then he was released with his own family and all his substance unto his own land. Why? 'Because they are my servants, which I brought forth out of the land of Egypt: they shall not be sold as bondmen' (Leviticus 25:42).

He reiterates in Leviticus 26:13, 'I am the Lord your God, who brought you forth out of the land of Egypt, that you should not be their bondmen; (slaves) and I have broken the bands of your yoke, and make you go upright.'

God was determined to avoid any form of exploitation and servitude amongst his own special people; as he said in the final verse, 'For unto me the children of Israel are servants; they are my servants whom I brought forth out of the land of Egypt: I am the Lord your God' (Leviticus 25:55).

As servants of the Lord, this was in regard to being a nation of holiness and teaching the other nations about the Lord with the oracles, instructions, and commandments. None of the 'gods' that the other nations served had that kind of setup!

There were occasions during their forty-year sojourn when they reflected upon their times in slavery when they ate garlic, leeks, cucumbers, onions, and melons, and complained about the manna that they initially enjoyed. They were not easily pleased!

Sadly, the chains of slavery were no longer physical but psychological; they were not worn on their hands and feet, but within their minds. They were on their way to the land of freedom as liberated people who were being refined. As things turned out, God still adhered to his promises, but they all perished in the wilderness with slavish conditioning and unbelief.

The Secret of Moseroth tells us that the chains of spiritual slavery, idolatry, discouragement, and unbelief, sin, and disobedience must be removed in the wilderness of testing. We can experience glorious freedom in Christ because he has freed us from the shackles of the law of sin and death.

We are encouraged under our training programme to 'Stand fast in the liberty wherein Christ has made us free, and be not entangled again in the yoke of bondage' (Galatians 5:1).

Slavish mentality and negativity cannot enter the land of promise.

Benejakan

Numbers 33:31-32 mentions Benejakan (meaning 'the wells of the children of Jaa-kan'), a campsite chosen for the Israelites on two occasions. Passing through this area, the people had ample water sufficient to water their flocks and children, cook, drink, and wash. How marvellous are the Lord's provisions. No one needs to be thirsty.

The secret of Benejakan tells us that Christ invites us to his well of living water that never runs dry. His invitation in Isaiah 55:1 is a call for everyone who so desires to drink deeply and be refreshed from their thirsty lives. There's enough for anyone and everyone.

Hor-Haggidgad

Numbers 33:32-33 mentions Hor-Haggidgad (meaning 'cleft mountain'). This was the thirty-third settlement where the people stopped. This place was probably a gully, a narrow channel or chasm, a deep cleft that the children of Israel had to safely cross over. This would mean assisting each other so that everybody was conveyed over. Vulnerable and older folk, pregnant women, and small children would have needed extra time and patience to climb over anything that lay ahead without endangering themselves. Those who were stronger would lift, carry, affirm, encourage, and help those less able to clamber over the ravine.

In comparison, there are times when we may need a physical, emotional, or spiritual helping hand in some form to guide us gently on our pathways. We need to work together as a team and be our brothers' keepers. As we venture along, there will be mishaps, hazards, and obstacles in our way to overcome. We should not turn our backs when the hindrance lies ahead in our path towards our destiny. When confronted with a problem, situation, or difficulty, we must endeavour, with the Lord's help, to be determined and press on with all our might, being fully dressed in the armour of his righteousness.

The secret of Hor-Haggidgad is that the path in the wilderness is smooth and easy to navigate but doesn't remain like that for too long. But we can be assured of God's assistance and that he will give us the grace we need sufficient to carry us through. If someone requires help travelling the same road, let us extend a hand of mercy and 'strengthen the hands, and affirm the feeble knees' (Hebrews 12:12).

Jotbathah

Numbers 33:33-34 mentions Jotbathah (meaning 'goodness'). Throughout the forty-year wilderness sojourn, God extended goodness to his people. Despite their complaints, he manifested the enduring patience of a merciful father. He bore them on 'eagles wings' (Exodus 19:4); he was their pillar of cloud by day, and a pillar of fire by night'.

And the Lord will bring you into the land which your fathers Abraham, Isaac and Jacob possessed, and you shall possess it; and he will do you good, and multiply you above your fathers.

If the children of Israel would obey the voice of the Lord and do his commands, then in return, ... the Lord they God will make you plenteous in every work of thine hand, in the fruit of they body, and in the fruit of your cattle, and in the fruit of your land, for good: for the Lord will again rejoice over you for good, as he rejoiced over your father ... (Deuteronomy 30:5, 9)

During a fast, Nehemiah addressed a different generation who happened to be in captivity, giving the account of God's mighty deliverance of the Israelites, beginning at the call of Abraham right up until they fully possessed the land of Canaan. 'You gave them also your good spirit to instruct them, and withheld not your manna from their mouth, and gave them water for their thirst' (Nehemiah 9:20).

The secret of Jotbathah tells us that God's goodness will follow us as we remain faithful to him. Abundant blessings will pervade every area of our lives, but obedience is key.

Ebronah

Numbers 33:34-35 mentions Ebronah (meaning 'gateway'). 'There is a way that seems right to a man, but it only leads to death' (Proverbs 14:12). God installed a visible leader, Moses, to deliver his people out of the land of satanic bondage and move them into a land that contained everything to sustain them. The first gateway was out of Egypt. The second gateway was through the wilderness, which led to the third gateway—the land of Canaan. These gateways were important for them to go through. There was to be no cheating, and there were no shortcuts.

Along their sojourns, they came along the borders (or gates) of Seir, the children of Esau, and were cautioned not to meddle or quarrel about their land. They were only given express permission to buy food and water for money. However, Edom were very hostile and inhospitable towards them, allowing no entrance through their territories but threatening them with the sword!

Other gates which they passed by were those of the Moabites; the Emins, who were giants; and the Ammonites. God did not forget their despicable actions, and later on in the scriptures we read about the prophecies of condemnation against those very nations in the books of Isaiah, Jeremiah, and Ezekiel.

The secret of Ebronah tells us that Jesus is both the Gate and the Door—the opener and closer of our destinies. In John 14:6, Jesus declares himself to be 'The Way, the Truth and the Life.' There are many other gates which lead away from the kingdom of heaven; operating through multiple faiths and practises, such as New Age, Catholicism, Islam, Hinduism, other eastern philosophies, and so forth. He carefully leads and directs all those who will follow Him through the narrow gate, which leads to eternal life.

Ezion-Gaber

Numbers 33:35-36 mentions Ezion-Gaber (meaning 'the backbone of a giant'). This temporary settlement was a town situated at the north side of the Gulf of Aqabah, near the Red Sea. Mentioned in several places in the scriptures, it was an important commercial seaport for smelting metals in the time of King Solomon. But more to the point, every experience that the children of Israel went through was to give them, as it were, the 'backbone of a giant.'

God had fought their enemies not only whilst they were in Egypt, but whilst they were in the wilderness too. They were soon to enter a land that was also filled with giants. The twelve men sent out to spy the land in Numbers 13 could assert that!

The path along the way of the Philistines was the shortest and quickest route to Canaan, but God did not want them to immediately engage in war. They were, after all, on testing ground.

Canaan 'was a land of giants ...' (Deuteronomy 2:20). 'A people great, and many and tall, as the Anakims' (Deuteronomy 2:21). The Moabites named the Anakims the Emims, whilst the Ammonites called them Zamzummims. And yet God was giving Israel that land with full authority and the ability to kick those heathen nations out and totally destroy them. In fact, those nations were mightier and stronger than them and were called the Amorites, the Perizzites, the Hivites, the Jebusites, the Hittites, the Canaanites, and the Girgashites.

The strangest irony behind this concept was that those other nations who had heard about the exploits of what this God had done in Egypt were terrified of this new people, Israel—unbeknownst to them. And although the Lord had encouraged them to be strong, the Israelites were also afraid of their enemies. Joshua and Caleb by faith entered the land with the new generation because they chose to believe that God had given them Canaan, armed with the confidence to eliminate the giants who dwelt there.

The Secret of Ezion-Gaber tells us that there is a giant in all of us and God wants us to develop confidence, inner strength, and perseverance, especially in our times of testing, in order that we may gain the emotional and spiritual resilience that will enable us to ride out any difficulties we may encounter not just in the wilderness but beyond as well—in the land of blessing. In addition, there will be battles to be won with testimonies of conquests and victories. Having the 'backbone of a giant' is what God fundamentally desires us to develop and exhibit. 'Because - Greater is he that is within me, than he that is in the world' (John 4:4).

Kadesh-Barnea

Numbers 33:36-37 mentions Kadesh-Barnea (meaning 'holy, sacred'). Journeying through the Sinai wilderness, the Israelites stayed and circled within the region of Kadesh on the outskirts of the wildernesses of Paran and Zin more than once. Seventy miles south of Hebron, this trip would have taken just eleven days to complete, had they been obedient in claiming the land.

Several events unfolded here. After doubting God's ability to give them the promised land, the Israelites were condemned to wander for a total of forty years until a new generation was completely formed (Deuteronomy 2:14).

In Deuteronomy chapter 2, Moses relates to the Israelites how he told them to go and possess the land. But since they were curious and needed more proof, they asked him to send men to search it out and give a report. Twelve men were sent from Kadesh-Barnea, and out of that scouting party just two gave an honest report, citing not only that it was a good land but also that the Lord was with them. The people needed not to dread or be afraid of them. And as for the ten men who gave a discouraging report, they died in the wilderness. Because they were unwilling to take the land, God added a further thirty-eight years to their wandering of the terrain until that entire generation had perished.

As the Israelites were nearing Canaan, King Arad heard about this powerful nation whose God had swallowed the Egyptians in the Red Sea and had shown mighty wonders in that land. Now they were approaching his territory, and he was terribly afraid. To shake them off, he made war with them and captured some as prisoners. According to Numbers 21:2, the people vowed to the Lord, saying, 'If you will deliver these people into my hands, then I will utterly destroy their cities.' God responded to their voice and gave them victory over their enemies, fulfilling their vow of total annihilation. The place was afterwards named Hormah (meaning 'destruction').

At this holy site, the congregation murmured and complained in their tents again. Their tears and their groans reached heaven as they spoke out against God, wishing they had died either in Egypt or in the wilderness. They further insinuated 'that the Lord had brought them into this land, to fall by the sword, that [their] wives and [their] children should be a prey.' They added, 'Let us make a captain and let's return back to Egypt!' (Numbers 14:3-4).

Moses ended up interceding on behalf of the people, but from that day on, their carcases fell in the wilderness, and all who murmured from twenty years old and upward died. Needless to say, the people regretted what they had said and mourned grievously. However, they didn't consider that they needed to accept their fate and move on. Instead they picked a leader and made an aggressive move to enter Canaan illegally, without the Lord's guidance or permission.

Consequently, the Amorites attacked them like bees; sending them packing all the way to Hormah.

At Kadesh, Miriam, the prophetess and older sister of Moses, died in the desert of Zin in the first month, Abib, and was buried there. She was the one who had led the people out of Egypt with songs of praise at the border of the Red Sea following her brother Moses's song. Those who remained would remember her shaking the timbrel and leading all the women into dances, saying 'Sing to the Lord, for he has triumphed gloriously; the horse and his rider he has thrown into the sea.' Now she had completed her run in the wilderness, and they mourned her loss.

Not long afterwards, the children of Israel cried out again for water to drink at this place. God, wanting to demonstrate his holiness in an unusual way, instructed Moses to just speak to the rock. But instead, in his anger (which had got him in trouble in the past), he took the rod which he was only meant to hold in his hand and struck the rock instead. 'Hear, you rebels; must we fetch you water out of this rock?' (Numbers 20:10). God was not glorified, but nonetheless he still gave the miserable people water to drink. Water mysteriously gushed forth from the rock, even though it was supposed to be spoken to. The people did not seem to recognize the significance of that act. They were so thirsty that they just drank without any concerns, and so did their animals.

Crucially, for Moses, there was a huge price to be paid for that error. He had, in that moment, failed to honour God and, as God put it, '... to believe me, to sanctify me in the eyes of the children of Israel, you shall not enter the land, which I have given them' Numbers 20:12).

Had God not responded by giving water on that occasion, it could have caused devastating repercussions for the people looking unto God to fulfil his promises and provision, and unto Moses as their leader!

Jesus Christ typified the Rock of Salvation, and we notice in the scriptures that he was struck on the face by the ruling high priest, as he underwent examination during his trial, prior to his death.

The secret of Kadesh-Barnea tells us much. This is the place where God's holiness was revealed, although on that occasion it wasn't executed in the way that it was supposed to be. Sanctification and obedience have immense significance, and the price tag is high for those who desire to come up higher in him. However, the rewards are immeasurable.

By refusing to lay claim to their stake by walking into their destinies, the children of Israel forfeited the right to their inheritance. Only the children and grandchildren were able to seize it instead. At Kadesh-Barnea, when God says 'Move', then we must move!

Moses learnt a painful lesson that he regretted for the rest of his life—especially when God excluded him from entering the Promised Land. It is so important to follow his directives, no matter how trivial they may seem. That way his name is glorified and he alone gets the praise.

Mount Hor

Numbers 33:37-39 mentions Mount Hor (meaning 'the hill'). It was at this location that Moses's eldest brother Aaron died and was buried. It was near the cleft mountains of Hor-Haggidgad. He too, like their sister Miriam, fell short of entering Canaan. He had walked through the entire journey with the people of God amidst the highs and lows of not just the desert terrain but also the tests and trials.

As high priest, he was influential in his office as mediator between God and his people, offering up incense and ensuring that all the official duties he executed were performed in righteousness and diligence. He was, after all, of Levitical ancestry.

God told Moses that Aaron would die in the wilderness not because he took part in making the golden calf but rather because he had ...'rebelled against my word at the water of Meribah' (Numbers 20:24). At his death, Moses was to bring Eleazar, his son, along; remove the priestly garments from his body; and place them on his son instead. Eleazar was installed as the next generation high priest.

The Bible gives us the date of his death and interment in verse 38. He was 123 years old when he died. He was buried on the hill of Mt Hor. It had been forty years since the children came out of Egypt on the first day of the fifth month. He was a well-respected man of God, and the people loved him and mourned his loss for an entire month before moving onward.

The secret of Mount Hor tells us that at some point on our travel towards our destination we will experience high levels of clarity. It rarely happens at the beginning of the journey, as things are new at that point and mistakes will be made. There will be personal triumphs and breakthroughs, and things will begin to become clearer, that deserve celebration and giving God praise. It may be an answer to prayer, a release in your spirit, or a long-awaited response to a request. It could be an open door towards an opportunity, healing, or a prophetic word for future reference. But whatever it is, it will be something that, in turn, we must give God thanks for and worship him for.

Things that are not of God need to drop off and 'die' on the mountain too, as he requires holiness.

Zalmonah

Numbers 33:41-42 mentions Zalmonah (meaning 'shady'). This was another desert camp after Mount Hor. The name suggests some gloomy valley leading to the Edomite plateau.

By that time, the vast majority of the people who had originally left Egypt and crossed the Red Sea had died. Conversely, the new generation who had been born in the wilderness were now making their way towards the land of promise.

This location doesn't suggest whether there were trees or anything that would give shade or covering to the people. It appeared that they found it extremely arduous ground. As a result, the people became very discouraged and found it difficult to hold their tongues. Once again, they approached the aged Moses and complained, saying, 'Why did you bring us out of Egypt to die in the wilderness? There's no bread here, nor water to drink, and our soul hates this light bread' (Numbers 21:5).

The people sounded despondent, miserable, and fed-up. Their words were laced with misery, regret, and ingratitude. Clearly this part of the terrain was difficult, but instead of remembering God's faithfulness and sustaining power, they took the opportunity to complain once again about their circumstances.

In the valley of despair, it's so easy to utter words of frustration when things don't make any sense at all. But hadn't God promised that he would never leave or forsake us?

The Lord responded by sending out fiery serpents among the people, which bit them, and many of the Israelites died. For those who were still wincing in agony and pain, they admitted their sin and begged Moses to intercede on their behalf to remove the snakes. God graciously replied by telling him to make a serpent of bronze and to set it upon a pole so that whosoever was bitten and looked upon the brazen serpent would then live.

The next time you walk past a pharmaceutical store, glimpse at certain types of medical packaging. Alternatively, look at any ambulance vehicle, paying close attention to the symbols on it. There is usually a cross with a snake coiled around the centre beam. From a biological point of view, those in the medical field, especially doctors and scientists, understand the true significance of the snake's bite; but do they really comprehend that the medical symbol (the snake on the pole) goes all the way back to the biblical incident found in the book of Numbers chapter 21?

The secret of Zalmonah tells us that tucked away amidst the gloom and shade of the wilderness, there is mercy for all. The sting of sin is death. The people had to look up to the same snake that bit them in order to receive life. The tale of the brazen serpent has become an integral part of the gospel ever since. When man confesses his need for deliverance from sin, he need only look up to the cross where Jesus died, to obtain forgiveness, grace, and life evermore. Whoever believes in Him shall not perish but shall have everlasting life.

Punon

Numbers 33:42-43 mentions Punon (meaning 'darkness'.) The children of Israel were inching ever closer to the land of Canaan, and at this desert settlement they came to a place which signified darkness.

Before leaving Egypt, the penultimate plague to strike there was the three days and nights of extreme darkness, which was so thick it could be felt. Intriguingly, whilst the Egyptians could not see one another or arise from their place, the Israelites enjoyed daylight hours in the dwellings of Goshen.

The darkness they were exposed to here was not, as a matter of course, related to the absence of light but to the likelihood of spiritual ignorance. The land they were heading towards was one that was to become holy. It was filled with nations whose demonic practices had desecrated it. The darkness of their sins were such that the Israelites were to totally destroy them, including the gods they served.

Whatever darkness the Israelites personally faced at this settlement, those sins needed to be completely eradicated. If they were walking in spiritual darkness, it was now time to open their spiritual eyes to the light of the truth of God's words, his promises, his instructions, and his commandments.

This new generation had seen the errors of their parents and the consequences for their unbelief. Now they had the opportunity to not only embrace the promises but also to live in such a way that would make their heavenly Father proud of them.

For the children of Israel, the darkness signified something far greater; the land of testing and sanctification was preparing them for something far beyond their wildest dreams. They were entering a land filled with better promises, new hopes, new life, new victories, new battles, new blessings and prosperity, posterity, and protection against those who would dare to fight against them.

At Jesus's death, darkness covered the land for three hours, from the sixth to the ninth hour. Prior to that, his last comment before giving up the ghost was 'Eli, Eli, lama sabachthani?' ('My God, my

God, why have you forsaken me?'). As much as he is God, in his humanity, God separated himself from his son because of the curse of sin that he took upon himself.

And yet this darkness signified something far much greater; his death meant completion over sin and the works of the flesh, ultimate victory over Satan, the blotting out of the handwriting of ordinances of the sacrificial laws—which also pointed to Christ—and power over death itself.

The secret of Punon tells us that the darkest hour is just before the day, and during those times, it seems as if all hell breaks loose. It may look like the sun won't shine any more—that it might seem unlikely that the things promised to you will ever be fulfilled—but he who promised is faithful (Hebrews 10:23). Remember, the darkness is the same as daylight to him (Psalm 139:12). When things seem black and bleak, we must still have the spiritual capacity to visualize the breakthroughs and promises beyond it.

When we cannot see our way through our situations, remember that 'The Lord is our light and our salvation' (Psalm 27:1). We are also reminded in Isaiah chapter 50, verse 10, that when we walk in the dark and have no light, we are to trust in the name of Lord and be confident in him.

Oboth

Numbers 33:43-44 mentions Oboth (meaning 'bottles'). This desert settlement was located just opposite (east) of Moab. It wasn't necessarily a location filled with bottles, although Matthew Henry in his commentary suggests that at Oboth they filled their bottles with water, because God had blessed them marvellously with water at the well or fountain at Beer, where they sang, 'Spring up, Oh well!' (Numbers 21:17).

I would like to insert the possibility of this being a reminder of all the numerous tears they had shed during their sojourns.

- Moses often cried to God when the people railed at him for food, water, replacement, and murmurings; when his leadership was challenged; and when they were being punished.
- They cried when they wanted water to drink (Exodus 15).
- They cried when the fire came down from heaven and burnt them for their complaining (Numbers 11).
- The mixed multitude wept when they reflected on the food in Egypt (Numbers 11:4).
- They cried when they heard about the giants in Canaan (Numbers 13:1).
- They cried when they were bitten by the fiery serpents (Numbers 21:8).
- They cried when they discovered that the water they drank from was bitter (Exodus 15).

In Psalm 56, verse 8, David muses and tells us, 'You count my wanderings: travels: put my tears into your bottle: are they not in your book?'

The tears they cried were known by God for what they were. Whether they were tears of sadness, anguish, regret, frustration, or misery, he recognized what those tears meant. There were so many instances where they cried and God responded to them through Moses and Aaron, time and time again.

The secret of Oboth tells us that no tears are ever wasted in the wilderness of testing, as long as we continue to believe his words and keep going towards our destiny. He carefully bottles our tears individually into bottles with our names on them. The tests are designed to teach us humility and total dependency on him. It's also a language he understands. There will be tears and sorrow in the wilderness, but one day they will be replaced with the oil of joy for mourning, and beauty for ashes. (Isaiah 61:3)

Ije-Abarim

Numbers 33:44-45 mentions Ije-Abarim (meaning 'the ruins of Abarim'). Geographically, this area was located on the eastern border within the plains of Moab, over one of the mountainous regions of Abarim. Other mountains nearby were Pisgah and Nebo, which overlooked the Dead Sea and Jericho.

The children of Israel had now cleared the wilderness environment and were facing Canaan from the rear position, viewing a plain which stretched with grazing grounds.

In Numbers 22–26, we are introduced to two main characters. Balak, son of Zippor, who was king of the Moabites, had heard about the fame of Israel and was intimidated by their vast numbers. He summoned a man called Balaam from Pethor in Mesopotamia. Described as a celebrated soothsayer, Balaam was well-known for his impressive abilities to effectively bless and curse. Interestingly, their names were very revealing too; 'Balak' means 'destroyer', and 'Balaam' means 'greedy'.

Balak desperately needed to employ Balaam's talents to curse and destroy this people, who, in his language, were like the 'oxen that licks up the grass of the field.' (Numbers 22:4). He promised to make him a very prestigious, wealthy man if he could fulfil his urgent importunity. On both occasions, he sent delegates to visit Balaam with honourable gifts to persuade him. After a consultation with God the previous night, he nonetheless, saddled his ass the next morning and made his own way to the king, even though God had already warned him not to. On his journey, the angel of the Lord withstood him three times with a drawn sword in his hand, and the ass turned away at each turn.

'And when the ass saw the angel of the Lord, she fell down under Balaam: and Balaam's anger was kindled, and he smote the ass with a staff. And the Lord opened the mouth of the ass, and she said unto Balaam, What have I done unto thee, that thou hast smitten me these three times: And Balaam said unto the ass, Because thou hast mocked me: I would there were a sword in mind hand, for now would

I kill thee. And the ass said unto Balaam, Am not I thine ass, upon which thou hast ridden ever since I was thine unto this day? Was I ever wont to do so unto thee? And he said Nay' (Numbers 22:27-30).

Balaam's lust for riches, had almost gotten him killed. After his conversation with the ass, the Lord opened his eyes to see the angel of the Lord, who cautioned him to only speak that God gave him to speak. (see Numbers 22:31-35.)

The king hurriedly prepared sacrifices of seven oxen and seven rams, upon seven altars high enough for them to visibly see the multitude, to which God responded by blessing his people twice through Balaam instead.

How shall I curse, whom God has not cursed? Or how shall I defy, whom the Lord has not defied? (Numbers 23:8).

God is not a man, that he should lie; or the son of man, that he should repent: has he said, and shall he not do it? Or has he spoken, and shall he not make it good? (Numbers 23:19).

Finally, Balak, out of frustration, told him not to bless or curse them at all. Balaam could relay only what the Lord had told him to speak. Then, without the use of enchantments, he blessed them and even predicted a time when the promised Messiah would appear: 'I shall see him, but not now: I shall behold him, but not nigh: there shall come a Star out of Jacob, and a Sceptre shall rise out of Israel, and shall smite the corners of Moab, and destroy all the children of Sheth.' (Numbers 24:17).

Balak was very disappointed that this blessed nation could not be destroyed, just as Balaam was disappointed that he wouldn't be given a handsome reward, as he had failed to deliver. Notwithstanding, he deliberately lured the children of Israel to get involved with the daughters of Moab. "And they willingly committed spiritual idolatry and fornication with them." The Moabites "called the people unto the sacrifices of their gods: and the people ate and bowed down to their gods. And Israel joined himself unto Baalpeor: and the anger of the Lord was kindled against Israel'" (Numbers 25:2).

Consequently, God sent a plague amongst the people, and the number of those that tragically died was twenty-four thousand.

This was the destruction of Abarim. Balaam was also killed shortly afterwards. The people were so close to entering Canaan, but yet again they missed out due to disbelief, idolatry, and disobedience. The people also represented those who were the complainers who left Egypt.

Attached to this story is another incident which occurred during the affliction of the children of Israel affiliation with the other countries of Moab and Midian, found within Numbers 25:6-15. It tells us about a prominent man named Zimri, from the Simeonite tribe, who blatantly took a woman called Cozbi, daughter of Zur, who was also from a prominent paganistic Midianite household, and had intercourse with her in his tent. As the congregation stood crying, Phineas, son of Eleazar, took a javelin in his hand to locate and kill them, whilst the plague was still decimating the people.

Zimri was fully aware of the caution God gave through Moses about being involved with pagan nations, including the Moabites, but he decided to disregard that warning. In the presence of Moses and the people, he was making a bold and defiant statement, and as a punishment, he was slain with the woman, with the javelin thrust through both their abdomens, and the plague was quenched.

Because of Phineas's brave and righteous act, God blessed him and his descendants after him in the priesthood.

The secret of Ije-Abarim tells us, to quote a passage of scripture,

'Wherefore seeing we also are compassed about with so great a cloud of witnesses, let us lay aside every weight, and the sin which does so easily beset us, and let us run with patience the race that is set before us. Looking unto Jesus the author and finisher of our faith ... (Hebrews 12:1–2a)

Although there are 'Baraks' who would try to destroy us, and the Balaams of the world who would try to curse us, God will ensure that neither of them can touch, harm, or hurt us. God will not curse those whom he has already blessed. As spiritual children of Abraham, we take on his DNA. As joint heirs with Jesus Christ, we take on his godly characteristics through the Holy Spirit.

I-im

Numbers 33:44-45 mentions I-im (meaning 'masses'). In Numbers chapter 26, we have the record of the second census of Israel. This time the census was taken in the plains of Moab by the River Jordan, overlooking Jericho. This ginormous task was again undertaken by Moses and his assistant Eleazar. They were to renumber the congregation aged from twenty years and upwards throughout all the tribes that were able to go to war in the land.

The total sum of them was six hundred one thousand seven hundred and thirty. Astonishing! The children born in the wilderness were now aged forty to account for the years spent travelling with their parents, and they had multiplied exponentially, like the sands of the earth and the stars of heaven, and yet the Levites were not numbered, nor the women, nor those under twenty (the grandchildren) and the children still to be born!

This was a very important census, as it determined who was given which portion of land once they had possessed it. Every detail was taken into account. 'To many you shall give the more inheritance, and to few you shall give the less inheritance: to every one shall his inheritance be given according to those that were numbered of him' (Numbers 26:54).

The secret of I-im tells us that, 'Eye hath not seen, nor ear heard, neither have entered into the heart of man, the things which God hath prepared for them that love him' (1 Corinthians 2:9). Every man will be rewarded for every deed done on this planet; whether it be good or whether it is evil.

Dibon-Gad

Numbers 33:45-46 mentions Dibon-Gad (meaning 'wasting'). In the exhortative song of Moses found in chapter 32 of Deuteronomy, the prophet rehearses the steadfast love of God concerning his relationship with the children Israel, reminding them of how they behaved towards Him all along the way. And in the following chapter, each tribe is prophetically blessed by Moses, the man of God, with words spoken similarly to those spoken by Jacob shortly before his death.

However, God told Moses to tell the people,

Your carcasses shall fall in the wilderness; and all that were numbered of you, according to your whole number, from twenty years old and upward, which have murmured against me. Doubtless you shall not come into the land, concerning which I swore to make you dwell therein, except Caleb the son of Jephunneh, and Joshua the son of Nun. But your little ones, which you said should be a prey, them will I bring in, and they shall know the land which you have despised. And your children shall wander in the wilderness forty years, and bear your whoredoms, until your carcasses are wasted in the wilderness. (Deuteronomy 14:29–31,33)

Those words met their exact fulfilment in Numbers 26 at the completion of the census. There was not a man whom Moses and Aaron the priest numbered when they numbered the children of Israel in the wilderness of Sinai during the first census, for the Lord had said that they would surely die in the wilderness.

Some more wasting occurred during the sojourn as the Israelites neared Canaan. There was the war against the Midianites, whereby one thousand men from each tribe were chosen for battle. Not only did they kill all the males, but they slew the five kings of Midian, took the women captive, and took their small children, cattle, flocks, and other goods. They burnt all their cities and all their goodly castles with fire. They took all the spoils and all the prey, both of men and of beasts, and brought them to Moses and Eleazar the priest. Moses instructed them to kill the females who had known a man but saved the female children. There was also the destruction of the king of Og, in the land of Bashan, and Sihon, king of Amorites, whom the children of Israel smote after they came out of Egypt. Now the people were learning how to fight and taking over territories to inherit their promised land.

The secret of Dibon-Gad tells us that when God promises to

bless and increase us, he attaches no sorrow (disappointment) to it. He will always keep his word. Just as the people increased in Egypt, so they increased in the wilderness. As his people, we can be assured that the blessings in the promised land will more than compensate for whatever we go through in the wilderness, even amongst the hardships.

At this junction, all our doubts, fears, misgivings, and insecurities must be wasted (destroyed) and dropped off at Dibon-Gad. Where there is immaturity, there should be maturity, accountability, and responsibility to take on the blessings that lie ahead.

Almon-Diblathaim

Numbers 33:46-47 mentions Almon-Diblathaim (meaning 'the concealing of the two fig cakes'). It was one of the last stopping places between Dibon-Gad and the mountains of Abarim.

The two fig cakes refer to the two most prominent figures of the exodus: Joseph and Moses. Their lives, in a sense—were good enough to eat! They had multiple godly 'ingredients', combined with a mixture of many hardships and temptations, which qualified them to play their roles exceptionally well.

Let's take a brief look at the beneficial aspects of the innocent fig fruit and then bring it into perspective regarding the two men. Figs are a good source of calcium and potassium, which can prevent osteoporosis and improve bone health and reduce bone turnover. They are also high in magnesium, zinc, and iron; aid digestion, helps manage blood fat and blood sugar levels; and kill cancer cells.

These good men accomplished a considerable amount for God's people and were both pivotal in the developmental shaping of Israel's history. They were individuals who were suitably selected by God as saviours for the nation's necessary survival and deliverance inside and outside of Egypt.

Hebrews 3:5 states, 'Moses verily was faithful in all his house, as a servant, for a testimony of those things which were to be spoken after.'

Both men were also born under special circumstances. One died and was buried just outside the Promised Land, whilst the other was actually buried there. Both men portrayed outstanding qualities of humility, integrity, obedience, diligence in service, resilience under pressure, and godliness.

Furthermore, their entire lives were lived out in the scriptures: Joseph's birth is recorded in Genesis 31; he then leaps to the age of seventeen from chapter 37 of Genesis right through to chapter 50. The life of Moses is charted from his birth to his death, from the books of Exodus straight through to Deuteronomy.

Fig Cake 1—Joseph

Rachel, Joseph's mother, had been barren for many years because God had closed her womb chiefly because of Jacob's ill treatment towards her sister, Leah, who was deceptively married to her husband first. But eventually God enabled her to become pregnant and gave her two sons, the first one being Joseph and the second being Benjamin.

Joseph was thrown into a pit by his brothers, purchased by the Ishmaelites for twenty pieces of silver, and taken down to Egypt. Just as the Israelites, he worked as a slave in the land of Egypt, away from his homeland and family. Employed by Potiphar, he was accused of sexual harassment by Potiphar's wife. He went into prison for a further decade and was made a prison officer by the prison warden. He was made prime minister of Egypt and created an economic programme to protect the country from death during the seven-year famine. Pharaoh promoted him to that high-ranking office because he was the only person found with the ability to explain and solve the meaning of his dream, with added practical solutions. He was given a new title: Zaphnath-Paaneah ('revealer of secrets'). He was also given a wife, a ring of authority, a chariot, new clothes, and a golden chain around his neck befitting his position. He was able to send for his entire family from out of the land of Canaan, which had also been severely affected by the famine, and he placed them in the best locations in Egypt—the fertile plains of Goshen.

Prior to his death, he made his brothers swear that when they eventually left the land of Egypt, they were to carry his bones along with them and bury him in the land of Shechem, located in Canaan, in a parcel of ground which Jacob their father brought from the sons of Hamor for one hundred pieces of silver. This became the inheritance of the children of Joseph, who were Ephraim and Manasseh.

It is worth noting that he was honourably embalmed and buried in Egypt, and after four hundred years of affliction, the tribes carried his bones along with them for another forty years through the wilderness before he was eventually laid to rest in Canaan.

When the children finally crossed into the land of Canaan, they were able to bury the first 'fig cake' (Joseph) in their allotted possession. He knew that his association was not tied up in the land of sin and bondage, though he had lived there for almost one hundred years (approximately ninety-three years in total), but his home was secured in the land of holiness and blessing.

Fig Cake 2—Moses

Moses was born at a time when the new pharaoh was in power, who did not know about Joseph and his achievements, and who was initially discouraged by the sheer size of the people of Israel. He firstly introduced hard labour, but when they continued to increase in numbers, he deployed a depopulation programme to reduce the masses. He told the midwives to kill all the male babies and cast them in the river, but to spare the baby girls.

Moses was found floating in a basket on the River Nile by Pharaoh's daughter. Weaned by his mother, he was taught about his identity. He was 'learned in all the wisdom and arts of the Egyptians, he was mighty in words and in deeds' (Acts 7:22). He was raised as a prince, living in the courts of Pharaoh, but his heart was with his people—the Hebrews. When he found out that Pharaoh knew that he had murdered one of his Egyptian men, he fled to the land of Midian, got married and had two sons, and was employed as a shepherd for the next forty years. One day God revealed himself to Moses, at the burning bush near Mount Horeb, and the rest is history.

Aged 120 years, Moses was coming to the end of his epic journey. At Mount Pisgah he gave a public charge in the presence of the children of Israel to Joshua to 'be strong and be of good courage: for you shall bring the children into the land which I swore unto them: and God will be with you' (Deuteronomy 31:23).

And now came the privileged and special moment for Moses to make his final climb to Mount Nebo to stand at the top of the hill Pisgah and view the spectacular landscape that he had so long desired to enter. The Lord granted him a private 360° panoramic tour and views of the land of Canaan, showing the allocations of Naphtali, Ephraim, Manasseh, and all the land of Judah; the south; and the plain of the valley of Jericho, (the city of palm trees) unto Zoar; Moab; and Gilead unto Dan.

Afterwards, Moses died in the valley in the land of Moab, against Bethpeor, 'but no man knows where his sepulchre is unto this day' (Deuteronomy 34:6) Even in the tiny book of Jude 1:9 we are told that 'Michael the archangel, when contending with the devil, disputed about the body of Moses.'

This, I daresay, is the hiding of the second 'fig cake.' However, no one knows where he was buried, because the Lord himself took care of his burial aspects. What is also fascinating is the fact that his face was not worn by time and age, and physically he was just as strong in his body to move and walk, and to have clear understanding and good memory in his mental capacities.

The new generation who had seen his leadership skills and his relationship with God mourned his loss for an entire month. This man, who bore characteristics similar to those of Christ, was often quoted. His dialogues and conversations with the people, in particular his debates with the scribes and Pharisees, were the usual sources of such quotations.

And after him there was none that God knew face to face, in all the signs and wonders, which the Lord sent him to do in the land of Egypt to Pharaoh, and to all his servants, and to all his land, and in all that mighty hand, and in all the great terror which Moses showed in the sight of all Israel. (Deuteronomy 34:10–12)

The secret of Almon-Diblathaim tells us that by taking a leaf from the godly lives of Joseph and Moses, we may live lives that are full of goodness and praiseworthy so that when we die, we may in return receive a glorious resurrection. May our lives be hidden in Christ in God, who is our life. 'If the same Spirit that raised Jesus from the dead dwells in you, he that raised up Christ from the dead shall quicken your mortal body by his Spirit, which dwells in you' (Romans 8:11).

Abarim

Numbers 33:47-48 mentions Abarim (meaning 'the mountains beyond'). Poised on the opposite side of Canaan, the new generation were being reminded of God's marvellous provisions in the wilderness and encouraged to be holy unto him. Moses was a very busy man— not just writing things down, but also reminding the people what they needed to do and what to prepare for. There was so much to remember!

Five months prior to Moses's death, there were still so many instructions to pass on and laws to be observed before crossing over into the land of blessing. At Abarim—the mountains beyond—they were told to secure six cities of refuge so that if a 'slayer, flee there, he may live …' (Numbers 35, Deuteronomy 19, Joshua 21).

It is interesting to note how keen Moses was to prepare and instruct the people for life on the other side of the wilderness, even though he knew that very soon he would die and leave them. He was faithful in rehearsing all the ordinances and commands for the people to follow. As a leader, he could have just disappeared and left them to their own devices after beholding their behaviour. Many times he had to negotiate with God and intercede on their behalf so God would not totally destroy them in his hot anger. But with fatherly, passionate concern, Moses patiently and strongly warned, exhorted, cautioned, and taught upon the mountains of Abarim.

There were laws to be observed in war: the use of the silver trumpets (Numbers 10:1–10), the dividing of the spoils (Numbers 31), and the redemption of the firstborn (Numbers 3). Moses strongly warned them to 'utterly destroy the nations' whose land they were to inhabit and possess (Deuteronomy 20:17). They were to destroy the graven images with fire, not even desiring the silver or gold that was on them, as it would be accursed. They were not to accommodate or spare idolaters, wizards, witches, prostitutes, fornicators, or any nation or person who could cause them to fall into sin.

In the case of the five sisters who had no brothers, God stipulated a law that included them in the inheritance of their father without depriving them of their rights as adult children (Numbers 27 and 36). Blood was forbidden to be eaten, and the worship of Molech was prohibited (Deuteronomy 12). They were reminded to observe the feast of Passover (chapter 16). Also addressed was what to do when a man wanted to divorce his wife (chapter 24), the power of vows (Numbers 30), marital issues (Deuteronomy 25, Ruth 3), giving the land her Sabbaths (Leviticus 26:32–43), the curses of the law (Deuteronomy 27:11–26), tithes and offerings (chapter 26:10–19), hygiene (chapter 23:10–15), animals, and exhortations to be obedient to the Lord (chapters 29–31). They were cautioned about what foods they were to eat and those they were to avoid (chapter 14), and circumcision was renewed once they had crossed over.

The Levitical tribes were not forgotten either. The book of Leviticus outlined all the ceremonial laws, sacrificial offerings, and other such matters, which they were to officiate and observe.

Once they had entered the land, they were to adhere to everything they had been taught as well as everything that had been spoken orally to them. The ordinances which were written down were also passed on so that they would not forget or get caught up in the paganistic cultures and immoral lifestyles of their sinful neighbours. The Canaanite civilisations were involved in objectionable practices, such as bestiality, child sacrifice, sexual immorality, body modification and branding, and the creation and worship of idols, which were (and still are) all abominable to the Lord.

They were also to teach and instruct their children how to love and worship the Lord so that when they were older they would continue those same traditions with their future families and descendants, within the same righteous framework that God intended for them.

[It was] Not for your righteousness, or for the uprightness of your heart, that you go to possess their land: but for the wickedness of these nations the Lord our God does drive them out from before you, and that he may perform the word which he swore unto your fathers, Abraham, Isaac, and Jacob. (Deuteronomy 9:5)

The secret of Abarim tells us that When we are on the cusp of a blessing (having scaled the mountain heights from the wilderness of testing and sanctification; and the valleys below), we must not slacken or get too comfortable. Remember the commandments of the Lord: they are paramount to your success in the promised land. And what he said to Israel he says to us too. He wants 'to make you high above all nations which he has made, in praise, and in name, and in honour; and that you may be an holy people unto the Lord your God, as he has spoken' (Deuteronomy 27:19).

Beth-Jeshimoth

Numbers 33:49 mentions Beth-Jeshimoth (meaning 'the house of deserts and wastes'). At this penultimate settlement, the people accounted for in the second census were taking territories even in the desert that pertained to the nations on the eastern side of Jordan. Although they still had many battles to conquer, those nearest to them were won with the almighty hand of the Lord.

Moses had reminded them at Mt Abarim, in the book of Deuteronomy, how they had dispossessed Sihon and Og and had utterly wasted those nations. The tribe of Reuben, the Gadites, and the half tribe of Manasseh were the first tribes who were able to rightfully claim the land they fought for on that side of Jordan (see Joshua 12:1–6). In fact, thirty-one kings in total were smitten over a period of time by the Israelites and are recorded in the same chapter of Joshua.

The tribes had approached Moses, as recorded in Numbers 32:16, and said,

We will build sheepfolds here for our cattle, and cities for our little ones: … We will not return unto our houses, until the children of Israel have inherited every man his inheritance. For we will not inherit with them on yonder side Jordan, or forward; because our inheritance is fallen to us on this side Jordan eastward. Our little ones, our wives, our flocks, and all our cattle shall be there in the cities of Gilead.

But before they could lay claim to their allotted lands, they were to help the other tribes. According to Numbers 32:29,

… Moses said to them, If the children of Gad and the children of Reuben will pass with you over Jordan, every man armed to battle, before the Lord, and the land shall be subdued before you; then you shall give them the land of Gilead for a possession: But if they will not pass over with you armed, they shall have possessions among you in the land of Canaan. They responded by saying, As the Lord has said to your servants, so will we do. We will pass over armed before the Lord into the Land of Canaan, that the possession of our inheritance on this side of Jordan may be ours.

The new generation of Israel were now pitched opposite the Dead Sea with one more hurdle to overcome. They had wandered for forty years until the previous generation were completely wiped out, in order to possess the land. They would soon exchange their tents for

… houses they did not build filled with good things, and wells already dug which they didn't dig, vineyards and olive trees, which they didn't plant. (Deuteronomy 6:11)

A land of brooks of water, … wheat, and barley and vines, fig trees and pomegranates, olives and honey; A land that you shall eat bread without scarcity … a land whose stones are iron, and whose hills you may dig brass. (Chapter 8:8–11)

This was probably their very last chance to ditch any preconceptions of bringing sin into the land with them. God had already foretold Moses how they would behave, and he communicated this to them by way of a dirge-like song as a perpetual reminder to their future generations.

Time and time again, Moses had constantly emphasized the importance of obedience and the remembrance of the Lord for his goodness. Don't forget him. Do not follow after the other nations' gods. In fact, the vast majority of the scriptures in the book of Deuteronomy tend to caution multiple times to '… fear the Lord your God, to walk in all his ways, and to love him, and to serve the Lord your God with all your heart and with all your soul.' (10:12) Two verses put it this way:

… if you do at all forget the Lord your God, and walk after other gods, and serve them, and worship them, I testify against you this day that you shall surely perish. As the nations which the Lord destroyed before your face, so shall you perish; because you would not be obedient unto the voice of the Lord your God. (Deuteronomy 8:19–20).

Most significantly with regard to the 'house of the deserts' is the story of a prostitute named Rahab, who took in two Israeli spies who were sent out by Joshua to spy out the land. Her cooperation was crucial to the total destruction of the city. She lived in Jericho, positioned within an encased part on the fortified wall of the town; and like the nations surrounding them, she, too, had heard all the stories about Israel's God, who had sent the plagues in Egypt, swallowed up Pharaoh's army, and devastated nations.

Although she lived in a land that was morally corrupt and worshipped foreign gods, she embraced the God of Israel by declaring, 'I know that the Lord has given you the land, and that your terror is fallen upon us, and that all the inhabitants of the land faint because of you … for the Lord your God, he is God in heaven above, and in earth beneath.' (Joshua 2:9,11)

Rahab, by faith, acknowledged the God of the Israelites and believed the reports she had personally heard. And although her house exposed her lifestyle as that of a woman of the night and everybody in the city knew who she was and what she did for a living, this same house of ill-repute became a temporary home of refuge to the spies, Jericho's enemies, and an 'ark' of salvation to her family.

The king of Jericho discovered that the men who came to spy out the land had also visited her house. She made a pact with the spies to deliver herself and her family from the destruction which was pending, by means of a scarlet cord which would be seen dangling in the window that she used to let the men escape from. (She might have heard the story of how Israel had daubed blood upon their doors). She hid them under some flax on top of the roof and gave the king's servants false intelligence, thus enabling the spies to return to Abel-Shittim without being found or killed.

In the meantime, she gathered her parents, siblings, and other relatives together under her roof until the Israelites came to destroy Jericho and their inhabitants. The only occupants spared in the city of Jericho were the residents found within the household of Rahab. Archaeological evidence reveals that her house, which faced the Judean wilderness, was not destroyed during the invasion and conquest of Joshua and the people of Israel.

In Noah's time, his preaching, unfortunately, did not save anybody; only his family of eight was spared. In this scenario, just one Gentile family from the entire city of Jericho was spared through Rahab's faith alone—the house of wastes.

Rahab, who was originally of Canaanite citizenship, eventually became linked to the Judaic royal ancestry of David by her marriage to Salmon, who produced Boaz. It was Boaz who famously married Ruth, the Moabite widow who produced Obed. Obed produced Jesse, who then produced David. His genealogy joins up right through to the lineage of Jesus Christ. Her name is also added to the distinguishable line-up of famous heroes and heroines in the well-known 'Faith' chapter of Hebrews 11.

The secret of Beth-Jeshimoth tells us that we will have to defeat all the devilish principalities that desire to rule our flesh, but God will decimate our woes, our foes, and our insecurities in the wilderness so we will have the strength to conquer and possess our new inheritance.

Sometimes in your walk, you may attract attention the attention of someone who would desire to know and embrace the same God that you serve, even whilst you're undergoing your hardships. You may never know who is watching your behaviour or 'listening' to your lifestyle.

Abel-Shittim

Numbers 33:49 mentions Abel-Shittim (meaning 'the meadow of acacias'). Joshua, approximately seventy years of age, was the new leader of the children of Israel and was now stationed near the embankment of the River Jordan with the children and grandchildren of Israel, who had been born in the wilderness. They had finally cleared the wilderness ground that had held so many poignant memories, crucial lessons, experiences, miracles, and tests, plus exhortations and instructions to retain.

The new generation of Israel stood at the brink of blessing, overlooking the land of promise. They could hardly contain their excitement! This was what their parents had travelled for. It was long anticipated and worth waiting for! Their legacy was within touching distance; they were almost there! And just as their parents had to cross the Red Sea to enter the testing ground, they, too, would have to cross over an expanse that separated them from their entrance into their destiny. Again, this would typify the death, burial, and resurrection into new life.

Let us look at some interesting facts about the River Jordan. The word 'Jordan' means 'descent; descender,' and the river is, according to website Britannia.com, 'more than 223 miles in length, but because its course is meandering, the actual distance between its source and the Dead sea is less than 124 miles.' Flowing southward into the Sea of Galilee, it empties into the mouth of the Dead Sea.

Mentioned over 185 times in scripture, it lies on the eastern border of Israel and the western borders of Syria and Jordan. It lies in a structural depression and has the lowest elevation of any river in the world. There are several instances in the Bible where the river plays a significant role. Naaman was cured there, and John the Baptist was frequently there. Jesus was baptized there, and it was there that Elijah and Elisha parted it with their mantle.

For most of the year, the river was about one hundred feet wide and only three to ten feet deep. But at the time of the Israelites' arrival, the River Jordan had overflowed its banks, and it was the time of harvest.

Before crossing over, the children of Israel required consecration, separation, preparation, and instruction. Let's break each of these words down.

1. Consecration: the Israelites were commanded to sanctify themselves, which included washing themselves and their clothes, and they were even forbidden to have intercourse with their wives. Why? Because the Lord would work wonders amongst them (Joshua 3:5). This would also require them to refrain from any activities which were normal but not essential.

2. Separation: they were all told to leave a gap of two thousand cubits between themselves and the ark of the covenant, which the Levites would carry ahead of them. (In our English measurement, this is equivalent to one thousand yards, or just over half a mile long.) To have that kind of distance would enable the Israelites—all three million of them—to see it visibly. When they wandered in the wilderness, the presence of the Lord was in the midst of them, but on this occasion he went ahead because 'you have not passed this before' (Joshua 3:4). They also had to recognize and respect the awesome presence of God—that he is holy and required that space.

3. Preparation and Instruction: There were instructions that needed to be followed if they were to reach the Promised

Land with the river as an obstruction. They needed to avoid disobedience to block their entry.

The Levites were to take up the ark of the covenant and go before the people. As soon as the feet of the priests dipped into the river, the waters would cut off from the waters that came from above, and they stood upon a heap. The priests had to take a step of faith and trust that God would deliver on his word by dipping their feet into the water. Joshua and Caleb, who had left Egypt, had crossed the Red Sea; now they were about to cross the Jordan's waters on dry ground, in a unique and supernatural way.

Twelve strong men, one from each tribe, were to take twelve large stones from out of the riverbed with them, placed upon their shoulders, and lodge in the land of Gilgal overnight. Each man wrote the name of the tribe on that stone; this would represent a continual memorial of their entry into the land of Canaan. They were also to tell their children, when they enquired, about the meaning of the stones, and explain how the God of their fathers enabled them to cross over Jordan on dry land.

The waters which came down from above stood and rose up upon an heap very far from the city Adam, that is beside Zaretan: and those that came down towards the sea of the plain, even the salt sea, failed, and were cut off: and the people passed over right against Jericho. And the priests that bare the ark of the covenant of the Lord stood firm on dry ground in the midst of Jordan, and all the Israelites passed over on dry ground, until all the people were passed clean over Jordan. (Joshua 3:16–17)

The Lord caused the waters to back up eighteen miles, all the way up to a location called the city of Adam, thus enabling the amazed crowd to cross over on a dried riverbed without drowning or accident. What a miraculous God!

The Lord spoke to Joshua and said,

Then you shall let your children know, saying, Israel came over this Jordan on dry land. For the Lord your God dried up the waters of Jordan from before you, until you were passed over, as the Lord your God did to the Red Sea, which he dried up from before us, until we were gone over; That all the people of the earth might know the hand of the Lord, that it is mighty; that you might fear the Lord your God forever. (Joshua 4:22–24)

And Joshua set up twelve stones in the midst of Jordan, in the place where the feet of the priests which bare the ark of the covenant stood: and they are there unto this day. For the priests which bare the ark stood in the midst of Jordan, until everything was finished. And it came to pass, when the priests that bare the ark of the covenant of the Lord were come up out of the midst of Jordan, and the soles of the priests' feet were lifted up unto the dry land, that the waters of Jordan return unto their place, and flowed over all his banks, as they did before. (Joshua 4:9–10,18)

The stones situated at Gilgal were left there as a memorial. They also served as a visual point of contact and powerful link to the manifestation of God, displayed at the bank of the River Jordan. The stones taken out by the twelve men had been made accessible only by the power of God.

Other notable facts deserve to be mentioned here: 'On that day the Lord magnified Joshua in the sight of all Israel, and they feared him, as they feared Moses, all the days of his life' (Joshua 4:14). God performed this feat not only to let to children know his power and might but also for them to recognize that he was with Joshua, their leader, just as he was with Moses, and that he was indeed appointed to lead them into the land and to assist them with their choice of allocations, and that during his leadership, God promised that no one would ever oppose or challenge him.

They were prepared for war. As soon as they crossed over— including the tribes of Rueben, Gad, and Manasseh—they selected forty thousand men to fight in battle within the plains of Jericho.

The date of their arrival in the Promised Land was in the year 1400 BC, on the tenth day of the first month, Abib. They crossed the River Jordan and camped in Gilgal, on the east border of Jericho.

With reference to the acacia tree, this place is commonly known as Shittim wood. Acacia trees grew abundantly in groups in the wilderness where the Israelites travelled. It was the only wood used in the construction of the tabernacle. The acacia is thorny with gnarly wood that changes grain. The yellow flowers of the tree are small and grow in clusters. It is not tall, and its trunk is thin and generally bent sideways.

Where the Israelites had stopped was a place filled with fragrant-smelling trees near the riverside. They were also in the area of the Moabites, who had deceitfully led the last of the ex-Egypt crowd astray into idolatry and whoredom.

In terms of durability and strength, this wood is resistant to decay, waterproof, and very fragrant. Insects also find it unpalatable. It was ideal for a tabernacle that would be moved around and transported during the forty-year sojourn. The beautiful acacia wood was used to make the altar of burnt offering, the altar of incense, and the ark of the covenant, all of which were overlaid with pure gold.

The secret of Abel-Shittim tells us that in the children of Israel's time, the ark of the covenant symbolized the immediate presence of the Lord. Today his fragrant presence will surround you in the land of blessing, joyfulness, and prosperity, just as he did in the land of Egypt and the wilderness. He will transform your life as you surrender to him completely in righteousness. His glory will take up residency within you as you keep your 'ark' (body) holy for his purposes.

Before we cross the threshold of greatness, we must be prepared to receive and obey the instructions of the Lord. Be consecrated and separated from anything that could possibly distract you from obtaining heaven's best. When Elijah was about to leave from his earthly assignment, Elisha stayed very close to him because he had seen his spiritual mentor's life and he needed that same kind of anointing. Together they passed through Gilgal, Bethel, and Jericho until they reached the River Jordan.

'Let a double portion of your spirit be upon me!' is a noble request to make to the Lord God before entering your destined inheritance. He will not deny the mantle of anointing and holiness to those who seek him in spirit and in truth. When we hunger for righteousness, we shall be filled!

For those who survive the extremes, the hazards, the pressures, the tests, the training, the lessons, and the instructions taught in the wilderness, the Holy Spirit will empower them to be Christ's ambassadors on earth.

Because you allowed the Lord to humble you in the desert and see his manifestation, he will exalt you, and 'he will let you ride upon the high places of the earth, and feed you with the heritage of Jacob your father' (Isaiah 58:14). After all, you are of Abraham's seed!

So there you have it. The wilderness terrain is designed to test your resolve and strengthen you spiritually, emotionally, and physically to help you to learn from your mistakes and give you instructions, practical guidance, and direction into ways that teach discipline, growth, and spiritual maturity; cleanse you for holiness; and prepare you to walk into your destiny proven and worthy of distinction. This is very personal; it is based upon individual merit and is all about developing a better you. If you can complete the course, then the dividends and rewards are substantial.

There are lessons to be learned, too—lessons of obedience; of how to trust, depend, and rest in the Lord; of walking in the dark; of loving the Lord; of leaning on his promises to remember his instructions as well as his promises; and of the knowledge of how to fight.

God wants us to develop godly character—evidence of righteousness—to increase our faith and build our relationship with him. He wants us to build resilience in our trials. He wants to instil patience and gain relentless endurance with all humility and wisdom. He wants us to understand that the challenges that lie ahead are far greater than those experienced in the wilderness, and that we need that kind fortitude to hold on to all those promises whilst tackling the hardships and tests there.

As parents, we can categorically agree that raising children is no mean feat! It is hard work complemented with good communicative techniques, education, training, instruction, corrective and disciplinary measures, and principles demonstrated with godly, loving, and parental care. Sometimes it may cause emotional heartache and pain for the 'guide' when a child chooses to stray from the correct course and decides to break the protective boundary, which could potentially lead to harm, pain, or destruction to himself or herself, or others.

The outcome of a child's progress will mostly depend on the child's willingness to accept those principles with obedience and humility, or resistance and constant rebellion. The path to holiness is not an easy one. That is why the way is narrow. But with persistence and by forming a relationship with God, it is very possible to follow that narrow path. Throughout the world, we have seen outward demonstrations of disobedience and its catastrophic results.

Equally, God was shaping his children, forging them in the fires of the wilderness backdrop, away from the public's prying gaze, with his unconditional love. The 'older' children were fully-grown adults, and yet they presented with childish, immature behaviour, which they could not seem to shake off during the forty-year trek. They were always complaining and crying when food and water were absent, murmuring about returning to Egypt, and playing up when given basic instructions.

Cynicism and doubt were definitely some of the main factors which ruined their chances of entering Canaan. Their hearts had become calloused to the messages of great expectations they received whilst travelling, and that made them resistant to transformation and hope, which would have kept them positive, confident, and alive.

Clearly, the wilderness programme is not for everybody! Yet it is a path that we must all pass through in order to reach to the other side. Many thousands died along the way due to unbelief. They often had their struggles, and they kept falling into that wide-mouthed trap of ingratitude; they even found it difficult to follow simple instructions given to help them along. Many were punished simply for grumbling and complaining. Only those who endured and passed the tests were able to move forward, embracing the promises: Joshua and Caleb and their families.

You will notice that the devil isn't mentioned throughout the trials; that's because God was doing the testing, not the devil. The people who refused to cooperate and did their own thing were tempted either by their pagan neighbours, who were influenced by the devil, or their own fleshly motives, and were subsequently punished for their actions.

We are further reminded by observation that our enemies do not disappear either; we just attract different ones. In all three areas—the land of Egypt, the wilderness, and the land of Canaan—there were foes that required elimination. God dealt with the cruel Egyptians, including Pharaoh and his army. He also destroyed the Amalekites, and the kings of Moab. In the wilderness, Israel's enemies gathered closer to them as they neared their destiny. They slayed many nations, and there were giants still awaiting them on the other side. Some they fought, and others they tolerated. The latter group, because of Israel's complacency about slaying them, became thorns in their sides.

One more reminder for the wilderness experience is that we can replace any thoughts of murmuring or doubts with singing. From Exodus to Deuteronomy, there is not a lot of singing or thanksgiving, but there is a lot of grumbling. In fact, after the episode of the Red Sea crossing, the only other song in this span is sung at the settlement of Oboth, when they collect water in their bottles. The people seemed to forget that they had been taken out of slavery and were on their way to better things. Let us learn to give God thanks in everything we go through, for in this he is well pleased.

We can rewrite our stories if we just reflect on the terrible mistakes and actions done by God's special people and instead choose to believe and take him at his word. There are other examples in scripture of individuals who chose to worship instead of being miserable. David is a classic example. His psalms are a treasure trove of spiritual delights filled with songs, supplications, meditations, prayers, and contemplative musings about his Maker. He filled his days with positive thoughts about God, about nature, and about praise to his greatness. Other contributors did the same. He also experienced times when he was distressed, anxious, worried, and downcast, which we can all identify with. Gratefully, we can borrow his anointed words and incorporate them into our devotional times of worship and prayers in any given situation.

As Egypt represents the world today, so too does Canaan, the land of promise, represent our heavenly home. Sandwiched between them is a life filled with hardships, health concerns, our families, financial worries, careers, relationships, toils, trials, and temptations for the child of God. This typifies our parallel wilderness journey, as we have not quite reached home—heaven—yet. However, at the end of the day, we will realize that all the sacrifices and commitments we make to find heaven will be worth it. And all that we need is in Jesus. He satisfies us, giving us joy and peace of mind. Life would be worthless without Him.

In closing, let us appreciate the testing ground of the wilderness that God sends our way to make us a people who will ultimately bring glory to his kingdom. May he give us the backbones of giants to conquer all our fears, resist temptations, slay our enemies, fight our battles, and anticipate new challenges with confidence and joy in our transition on the other side of the wilderness. Boot camp training is finally over, and an exciting, glorious future lies ahead. Welcome to Canaan!

Blessed by the God, and Father of our Lord Jesus Christ, which according to his abundant mercy has begotten us again unto a lively hope by the resurrection of Jesus Christ from the dead, To an inheritance incorruptible, and undefiled, and that fades not away, reserved in heaven for you,

Who are kept by the power of God through faith unto salvation ready to be revealed in the last time. Wherein you greatly rejoice, though now for a season, if need be, you are in heaviness through manifold temptations: That the trial of your faith being much more precious than of gold that perishes, though it be tried with fire, might be found unto praise and honour and glory at the appearing of Jesus Christ: Whom having not seen, ye love; in whom, though now you see him not, yet believing, you rejoice with joy unspeakable and full of glory;

Receiving the end of your faith, even the salvation of your souls.

Forasmuch as you know that you were not redeemed with corruptible things, as silver and gold, from your vain conversation … But with the precious blood of Christ, as of a lamb with blemish and without spot: Who verily was foreordained before the foundation the world, but was manifest in these last times for you.

Being born again, not of corruptible seed, but of incorruptible, by the word of God, which lives and abides forever. (1 Peter 1:3–9, 18–19, 23)

Printed in Great Britain
by Amazon

49362079R00135